Jan Compagnie in the
Straits of Malacca,
1641–1795

Jan Compagnie in the Straits of Malacca, 1641–1795

Dianne Lewis

OHIO UNIVERSITY CENTER FOR INTERNATIONAL STUDIES

MONOGRAPHS IN INTERNATIONAL STUDIES

SOUTHEAST ASIA SERIES NO. 96

ATHENS

© 1995 by the
Center for International Studies
Ohio University

Printed in the United States of America
All rights reserved
02 01 00 99 98 97 96 95   5 4 3 2 1

The books in the Center for International Studies Monograph Series
are printed on acid-free paper ∞

Library of Congress Cataloging-in-Publication Data available
ISBN 0-89680-187-x
Southeast Asia series No. 96

For Nicholas Tarling

Contents

Preface

This work is a revision of a thesis accepted by the Australian National University for a Ph. D. degree in 1971. The thesis was entitled *The Dutch East India Company and the Straits of Malacca, 1700–1784*. Chapters 2 and 5 have appeared in earlier versions; the former appeared as "The Last Malay Raja Muda of Johor," *JSEAS* 13.2 (1982): 221–35; and the latter as "The Growth of the Country Trade to the Straits of Malacca, 1760–1777," *JMBRAS* 43.2 (1970): 114–30.

In the long interval since the acceptance of my thesis I have altered the main thrust of my work, excluding much general material on trade in favor of a more succinct account of the operations of the VOC in the area for the whole period of their occupation of Malacca, from 1641 to 1795. My interest has, however, remained centered on the history of the Straits of Malacca rather than that of the Dutch Company, and in the following work I may have succeeded in pleasing neither the devoted historians of the Company, nor the historians of Malaysia. However, I am convinced that it is a story worth the telling, and so I offer it without apology, except in that it has been so long in coming.

In the interval I have had the opportunity to discuss this theme with many people, all of whom I am immensely grateful to for bearing with me and helping to keep my interest in Southeast Asian history alive. I cannot thank all of these people individually, but must especially acknowledge the generous help and advice of Virginia Matheson, Anthony Reid, Nicholas Tarling, Barbara and Leonard Andaya, and Eva Vanicek in Australia and New Zealand; John Bastin and David Bassett in England; and Oliver Wolters, Audrey Kahin, Carl Trocki and Lorraine Gresick in the U.S.A. Such virtue as is to be found in the following pages owes much to them. Any faults and errors are mine alone.

Since I began this study I have been privileged to use material in the Menzies Library, at the Australian National University, Canberra; the

Rijksarchief in The Hague, Holland; the India Office Library, and the Reading Room of the British Museum, (now the British Library), London; the Arkip Nasional in Kuala Lumpur, and, most recently, the Wason collection in the Olin Library at Cornell University. I wish to record my thanks to the staff of them all. In all of these places I have received much help and encouragement. Finally, I must thank the University of Queensland for granting me the Walter and Eliza Hall Travelling Scholarship, which allowed me to work in the Rijksarchief in 1969–71; and to my family, which has over the years borne tolerantly with an unemployed but still obsessed historian.

Dianne Lewis, Puerto Rico 1993

Note. I have tried to incorporate recent work on this subject to bring it up to date. Reinout Vos's work on Malacca, *Gentle Janus, merchant prince,* Leiden, 1993, only came into my hands after I completed and submitted the final manuscript, and is not referred to here.

A Note on Spelling

The author has taken the 1982 edition of the *Tuhfat al-Nafis,* prepared by Virginia Matheson and Barbara Watson Andaya, as a standard for the spelling of Malay and Indonesian place and proper names used in this text.

Abbreviations

BKI	Bijdragen tot de Taal- Land- en Volkenkunde van Nederlandsch-Indie
f	guilders (Dutch unit of currency)
JIA	Journal of the Indian Archipelago
JMBRAS	Journal of the Malay Branch, Royal Asiatic Society
JRAS	Journal of the Royal Asiatic Society
JSBRAS	Journal of the Straits Branch, Royal Asiatic Society
JSEAH	Journal of South East Asian History
JSEAS	Journal of South East Asian Studies
Kol. Arch.	Koloniaal Archief; prefixes registry numbers of correspondence of VOC in archival references
MBRAS	Malay Branch, Royal Asiatic Society
rds	RijksDollars; unit of currency of the VOC, worth about $Sp.0.8 or *f*2.5 (amounts vary with time)
Sp $	Spanish Dollar, or Real of Eight; favorite currency of the East Indies in the eighteenth century; worth about *f*3.2
SFR	Sumatra Factory Records
SSR	Straits Settlements Records
TBG	Tijdschrift voor Indische Taal- Land- en Volkenkunde
VOC	Verenigde Oostindische Compagnie
VKI	Verhandelingen van de Koningklijk Instituut voor Taal- Land- en Volkenkunde

Jan Compagnie in the
Straits of Malacca,
1641–1795

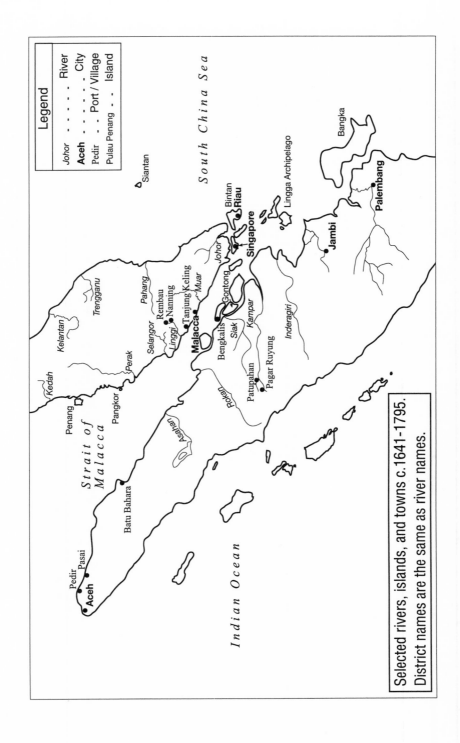

Legend

Johor - - - - -	River
Aceh - - - ●	City
Pedir - - ●	Port / Village
Pulau Penang - ▫	Island

South China Sea

Siantan

Bintan
Riau
Singapore
Lingga Archipelago

Bangka

Palembang

Jambi

Johor

Pahang
Rembau
Linggi *Nanning*
Tanjung Keling
Muar
Malacca
Gontong
Bengkalis
Siak
Kampar
Patupahan
Pagar Ruyung
Inderagiri

Selangor
Perak
Trengganu
Kelantan
Kedah
Penang
Pangkor

Rokan

Asahan

Strait of Malacca

Batu Bahara

Pedir
Pasai
Aceh

Indian Ocean

Selected rivers, islands, and towns c.1641-1795. District names are the same as river names.

Introduction

MALACCA IN MALAY
HISTORY TO 1641

No GENERATION ever learns quite the same history as its parents or its children. An older generation of historians saw Malay history in terms of the progress of European rule, and interpreted the few facts available to that end. Growing up in a postwar atmosphere of anti-colonialism, I was more interested in the effects of this encroachment of an alien power on the Malay world. The following is not a history of the Dutch colonization of the Straits of Malacca. It is an attempt to show how the Dutch became increasingly involved in the area by the very fact of their presence, and how this alien presence undermined the delicately balanced political structure that had sprung from the unusual combination of demographic instability and abundant foreign trade.

For a century Malay Malacca was the queen city of the Malay Archipelago, one of the great trade centers of the world, dominating traffic through the Straits that still bear her name; a place, in the words of the Portuguese Tomé Pires, who saw her in her glory, "at the end of the monsoons, where you find what you want, and sometimes more than you are looking for."[1] Merchandise from Arabia, Persia, India, China, the Malay Archipelago, and even such distant corners of the world as Portugal and Japan could be found in the marketplace of Malay Malacca. In the early sixteenth century the Portuguese came to this city; they were followed a hundred years later by the Dutch. These

Europeans saw in Malacca more than a marketplace; for them, the port was a symbol of the wealth and luxury of Asia, wealth and luxury that had lured them halfway around the world in their tiny, uncomfortable vessels. The Portuguese attacked and captured Malacca in 1511, hoping to capture also all it stood for. This was of course an impossible dream, and the trade of Asia continued around them, disturbed only marginally by the aggression of this handful of outsiders. Nevertheless, their act had important consequences; the capture and continued occupation of the port-city of Malacca by Europeans throughout the sixteenth, seventeenth, and eighteenth centuries had a highly significant effect on the history of the Malay people, massively disrupting their economic and political organization and contributing largely to their inability to meet the new challenge of industrialized European nations in the early nineteenth century.

Malay Malacca was itself only one in a progression of port-cities that had flourished and died on the shores of the Straits of Malacca. These Straits, homeland of the Malay people, lie between the island of Sumatra and the southeastern tip of Asia, the Malay Peninsula. Today these waters mark the political boundary of the modern states of Indonesia and Malaysia, and the latest of these great port-cities, the independent state of Singapore, lies at their southern entrance. Both the port and the boundary are legacies of the division of the Straits into English and Dutch spheres of influence in the nineteenth century. Before that time the Straits presented neither physical nor political barriers to the various Malay polities that flourished along their shores, for the land rather than the water was terra incognita to the Malays, and the ports served to focus and nourish these sea-oriented communities. The warm, shallow, island-strewn waters of the Straits, flanked on either side by low mangrove swamps through which meandered the mouths of large river systems, were familiar territory to the people who lived by their shores. The sea brought wealth, while the tropical rainfall quickly leached any goodness from the patches of sour, lateritic soil cleared from the jungle. The jungle and the sea, rather than the soil, provided a living for the inhabitants of the Straits of Malacca, the people who called themselves Malay. They were early among the great sea-faring peoples of the world, travelling as far afield as Madagascar and the Pacific islands before Europeans dreamed of the existence of such places. As international trade increased, Malay seamen soon became employed in long-distance trade. By the third century A.D., Malay shipping had itself begun to play an important part in the traffic through the Straits, carrying to China, among other things, the precious incense of Persia and Arabia.

The calm waters of the Straits provided a relatively safe sea route between the great civilizations of India and China. The Malacca Straits had become important to inter-Asian trade by the second century A.D., after the land route had been disrupted by warfare. A kaleidoscopic procession of merchants and soldiers, pilgrims and scholars passed this way, and with them the baggage, cultural and material, brought from many distant lands. The passage through the Straits was not swift, but it was certain—the prevailing monsoon winds could be relied upon for both the outward and the homeward leg of the voyage to the east or the west in alternate halves of the year. But there was always a delay, waiting on the winds, so vessels from western Asia did not usually continue to China, and their cargos had to be trans-shipped. Ports grew up first at the northern end of the Straits, on the Isthmus of Kra, where goods could be hauled overland to the China Sea by the shortest possible route. Later, ports appeared also to the south, on the coasts of Java and southeast Sumatra, as ships from the west ventured further afield. In the fifth or sixth centuries merchants found that the pine resin and benzoin from the jungles of Sumatra could be substituted profitably for the costly Arabian incenses that were in such high demand in China, and so profits from a local collecting trade were added to those won by catering to the through trade.[2] This made the southern Sumatran ports even more attractive. Over the centuries many ports emerged along the coasts of the Straits, and a few acquired great wealth. This wealth was used to support increasingly sophisticated societies and forge extensive political connections, to encourage the people of the hinterland to supply provisions and trade goods to the port's community, in return for wealth and a chance to participate in the growing mystique of the rulers of the major commercial centers. Thus the port-city became basic to the political structure of the Malay world.

The main assets of such a city were its position, its population, and its ruler. Of the three, the quality of the ruler was arguably the most vital. In an area where flood or fire could wipe out a port in short order—or, if it so desired, half the town could pack up and sail away overnight—the power of the ruler to attract and retain followers, and wealth in the form of shipping, was all-important. The power and prestige of the community became vested in the ruler. Little wonder, then, that a collection of myths grew up surrounding the most effective of these figures.

Contact between the travellers and the local communities was not always peaceful—the very nature of the Straits makes them an ideal place for marauders as well as peaceful traders. There is a long and continuing history of "piracy" by local chiefs who were overly ambitious, or out of favor with the current Malay power structure, or were, perhaps, trying to establish the predominance of their own port. Such renegades were frowned on by the ever-more-powerful rulers of the port-cities. It was in the interest of this latter group to encourage trade by ensuring the safety of the waterways. Such factors engendered the growth of a complex socio-political structure around the port-cities, as their rulers strove to attach the communities of the hinterlands and surrounding coasts to themselves by economic and religious means. The relationship of the cities with the international traders was symbiotic rather than parasitic, and their success both depended on and contributed to the prosperity of the passing merchants.

During the seventh century, Srivijaya, a Buddhist port-city whose site lay somewhere near present day Palembang on the southeast coast of Sumatra, emerged as the dominant political entity in the Straits. At the height of its power Srivijaya claimed overlordship not only of the coasts of Sumatra and the Malay Peninsula, but also of Western Java, the Sunda, and the Malaccan Straits. Its Rajas claimed divine descent. For six centuries Srivijaya—or Palembang, the name it appears to have been know by in later times—was the trade center of the Malay world, dominating contact between India and China. The magnificence of the Sumatran power was to remain fixed in Malay cultural memories long after changes in the trade patterns led to the collapse of its empire and the obliteration of its capital sometime in the twelfth or thirteenth century.[3]

The sophisticated socio-political structure that the Malay world had developed by the time of Srivijaya/Palembang was based almost exclusively on the wealth drawn from the passing international trade. It cannot be stressed too often that though the years had increasingly taught the people of the Straits to profit from the bounty of the jungle, this was basically a poor area. The soil of the Straits' coasts is not rich—where the jungle is removed it quickly loses all fertility—leached by the heavy tropical rain. In most periods food had to be imported from the more fruitful Menam and Irrawaddy deltas, and from fertile Java. Jungle products, tin, and some gold could be sold at profit to the foreigners; later pepper was cultivated in the more agriculturally favored areas of Kedah and the valleys of north and south Sumatra. The only substantial wealth in the Straits was brought by the foreign merchants. This left the Malay rulers open to the vagaries of international trade. The decline in the external trade from China in the twelfth century cut off the flow of wealth to Srivijaya, and led to the collapse of its empire and decades of lawlessness in the Straits of Malacca.

In the early fifteenth century, reviving interest on the part of the Chinese in the products of the south seas encouraged the rise of its successor. The port of Malacca, founded by a prince who claimed descent from the Palembang line, had two great advantages over the other ports that had grown up during the years of the old empire's disintegration— the favor of the Chinese Emperor, and a series of rulers who exerted all their considerable organizational skill and determination to make their port the center of the trade not only of the Straits, but of the whole Archipelago—one might almost say, of the whole of Asia.[4]

We know little or nothing of them as men, but a great deal of them as rulers. We know that they took great care to attract foreign merchants to their port; that every possible step was taken to make the new port attractive to the passing trade. A special governing body and judicial system gave them and their goods protection while in the port. The main officials of the court, the Bendahara, Laksamana, Syahbandar, and Temenggung were all responsible in one way or another for facilitating the business of the foreign trader.[5] Malacca's port regulations were designed to speed up the necessary processes involved in exchanging goods, so that merchants could dispatch their cargos rapidly, and long voyages would not be made even longer by the loss of the appropriate monsoon. Regular customs duties were established, systems of fixed weights and measures and of coinage were adopted. The sea-lanes around Malacca were patrolled by strongly manned vessels powered by oar rather than sail, so as to be able to tow becalmed vessels into port. Adequate warehouses were provided for those goods that had to be stored while waiting trans-shipment.

All of Malaccan society was involved in this quest to woo the passing trade. The Malay nobles did not themselves take an active part in trade, leaving this to the merchants from India and elsewhere, but they protected it. They commanded the fleet that policed the foreshores of Malacca and kept them free from the piracy that had been endemic in the Straits since the fall of Srivijaya.

The Malaccan rulers were equally skillful in their alliances. Malacca's founder, following the opportunities opened to him by the visit of the Chinese envoy Cheng Ho in 1403, readily accepted Chinese overlordship. He and his immediate successors sent tribute to China, and were rewarded with lavish gifts, establishing a special kind of trade, the Tribute trade, which ensured that Malacca would be known for its supplies of Chinese goods. Malacca's rulers personally travelled five times to China with their gifts, to cement this new friendship. But in the course of the fifteenth century Chinese interest in the outside world gradually died out once again, and the Emperor banned the private trade to the South Seas. The third Malaccan ruler, travelling to China with a Chinese fleet in 1433, was made painfully aware that he would have to turn elsewhere to insure the survival of his port. He was equal to the challenge, however, and managed to attract the important trade of the Indian merchants, a largely Muslim group which had formerly frequented the Islamic ports of northern Sumatra. He also wooed the Javanese. To this end he took the initiative and adopted the religion of Islam in place of the old Buddhist faith of Srivijaya to attract these Muslim traders.[6] The move must have been successful, for in the following decades Malacca entered a period of great prosperity.

Malacca's trade in its heyday was all that its ambitious founders could have desired.[7] There was heavy traffic from western Asia; Indian shipping came regularly from the Gujarat and Coromandel Coasts, Bengal and Pegu, bringing merchants from as far afield as Ethiopia and Armenia, and goods from even farther. These goods included luxury items from the Middle East such as rosewater, incense, opium, and carpets, as well as seeds and grains; but the bulk of the cargos were made up of cotton cloth from the Gujarat and Coromandel coasts of India.

Vessels from Bengal brought foodstuffs: rice, cane sugar, dried and salted meat and fish, preserved vegetables, and candied fruits, as well as the local white cotton fabrics, while Malabar merchants brought pepper. Pegu also supplied foodstuffs, rice and sugar, and ships. In return spices, gold, camphor, tin, sandalwood, alum, and pearls, were sent from the Archipelago; porcelain, musk, silk, quicksilver, copper, and vermilion were trans-shipped from China. Malabar or Sumatran pepper was carried back to Bengal, with some opium from the Arabian countries.

There was an equally important trade to and from the East; both official Tribute trade to China and unofficial junk trade, carrying large quantities of raw and woven silks, damask, satin and brocade, porcelain and pottery, musk, camphor, and pearls, as well as the less valuable alum, saltpeter, sulphur, copper, iron, and copper and iron utensils. Shipping also came at times from Siam, Indo-China, Japan and the Philippines, contributing foodstuffs, jungle goods, and a variety of other items.

The trade within the Archipelago itself had by now become highly profitable, as the spices of the Moluccas, nutmeg, mace, and cloves, had gained worldwide importance. The Javanese from the Muslim ports of the north coast were foremost in inter-Archipelagan trade. Other products of the Archipelago were foodstuffs, jungle products, and poor quality gold. From the Straits area itself, notably from the inland territory of Siak, and from Kedah, Pasai, and Pedir on the northwest coast of Sumatra came tin, gold, jungle products, and pepper, in return for cloth, opium, and, probably, foodstuffs.

> All these people bring so much wealth, both from East and West, that Malacca seems a centre at which are assembled all the natural products of the earth, and the artificial ones of man. On this account, although situated in a barren land, it is, through an interchange of commodities, more amply supplied with everything than the countries themselves from which they come.[8]

By the end of the fifteenth century, when the first Portuguese came creeping round the southern tip of Africa in their tiny galleons, eager to circumvent the monopoly of Venice over the priceless spice trade, Malacca had become the trading hub of Asia. Many of our best descriptions of this bustling city come from the Portuguese, whose home ports in the far Atlantic, away from all the major trade routes, must have seemed poor and provincial by comparison to cosmopolitan Malacca. Poorest of all the foreign merchants to come to Malacca, except in technology, the Portuguese decided almost at once to use their one advantage to capture the riches of the trade of Asia. They would conquer some of the major trade centers and, with their superior sea power, force all the rich trade to these ports. Malacca was a prime target.

The Portuguese accomplished the physical capture of Malacca in 1511, overcoming Sultan Mahmud's vastly superior forces with remarkable ease.[9] Many factors underlay this victory; perhaps the most vital being that the Portuguese were a small, cohesive band, singleminded and ferocious in their desire for glory.[10] But their main advantage lay in dissension in the Malay camp, for the reigning Sultan, Mahmud, was not as capable as his predecessors, and had alienated important sections of the Malaccan community by his execution of the powerful Bendahara, the chief minister of the Malaccan court, who had strong links with the Indian merchants.

The Portuguese also enjoyed the advantage of surprise. Mahmud can hardly have been expected to take very seriously the threat posed by a handful of poor "Frankish" adventurers from the ends of the earth. From a Malay point of view, the European attack on the port of Malacca could have made little sense. To the Malays, the essence of Malacca's power was not its physical location, but its social superstructure, the court and its ruler. A number of ports had arisen over the years, and though Malacca was a useful and favored site, it was only one of many; the trade did not flow to it automatically. The ruler attracted the trade to the port. The hinterlands were not bound to the physical site of Malacca, but to its ruler. Mahmud's power came not because he ruled the scrap of ground called Malacca, but because he was the descendent of the line of the rulers of Palembang, who had by then been invested with mystical origins of great significance to their subjects. This was to remain an essential difference in Malay and European thinking—the Portuguese, and later the Dutch, believing that they had won tangible "rights" to the trade of the Straits by virtue of the capture of the physical site of Malacca, while the Malays knew that this trade came only to those ports which were successful in wooing it, and that an important element in the wooing was the existence of a traditional ruler of powerful lineage.[11]

Which is not to say that the capture of the town of Malacca was not a great blow to the immediate material power of Malacca's ruler. The disruption caused by the Portuguese attack was critical because of the very strong connection between trade and politics in the Malay polities. Land was of little consequence in reckoning status. Population and wealth were the denominators—and wealth often dictated population, for Malay demography was notoriously fluid, the seas and rivers offering an easy means for whole communities both to move at will and to provide a living for themselves wherever they moved. The ruler of a rich port could attract many followers if his wealth was cannily distributed. Wealth in itself was an attraction, for its possession implied an almost mystical power. And the accumulation of wealth in the Straits of Malacca was tied to the control of an attractive and prosperous port.[12] Deprived of the port that had taken his ancestors decades to develop, Mahmud was at an immediate disadvantage in the competition to attract trade, and the machinery that bound his subjects in the hinterland to him was badly strained.

Sultan Mahmud's immediate reaction to the loss of Malacca was to attempt to draw the shipping en route to Malacca from Java, China, and the East to the site of his new court. He had fled south, first to the island of Bintan, then to the mouth of the Johor River, which presently gave its name to a new state. Here he was able to intercept some of the westward trade before it entered the Straits.

Instead of capturing Malacca's trade, the Portuguese had fragmented it. They also labored under another handicap—their Christian religion, which was most unpalatable to the Muslim merchants of India and Java. Many of the latter preferred to deal with the Malays of Johor, and the Indians began to make for the hitherto obscure but fervently Muslim port of Banda Aceh in the north of Sumatra, despite the fact that this port was cut off from easy access to Chinese trade by the Portuguese at Malacca. Moreover, the Portuguese had violated a fundamental condition of Malacca's attraction to the passing trade; for their act turned the Straits into a battlefield. The Malays could not rest content while Portuguese ruled the port. In the sixteenth century Johor mounted major attacks against Malacca in 1517, 1520 and 1521, the northern Sumatran kingdom of Aceh followed suit in 1558, 1570, and 1575. Even the Javanese state of Japara attacked the Portuguese port in 1574.[13]

Rivalry between Johor in the south, trying to re-establish Mahmud as the premier ruler of the Malay world, and Aceh in the north, fueled by its ever growing trade with India, added to the increasing turbulence of the area.

The Portuguese also drove trade away from Malacca by their attempts to regulate it for their own profit. For instance, Chinese shipping was at first encouraged to continue to frequent Malacca, but, as the Portuguese extended their commerce in Asia, they decided that Chinese trade at Malacca was detrimental to their own factory at Macao. The "pass" system instigated by the Portuguese, requiring merchants to obtain permission from the Portuguese before proceeding with their voyages to the surrounding ports, on pain of having their vessels and cargos confiscated by patrolling Portuguese warships, was the very reverse of the policies pursued by the founders of Malacca. This Portuguese attempt to monopolize Asian trade relied on their superior sea-power, and sought to channel Asian merchants to Portuguese ports to maximize those ports' wealth. But the volume of shipping greatly exceeded their ability to police it, and their efforts probably contributed to, rather than prevented, the disintegration of Malacca's position as the main entrepôt of the Archipelago.[14]

Malacca did not lose all its trade to its rivals. In the sixteenth and seventeenth centuries the abundant trade that had led to the establishment of Malacca continued to flow through the Straits, and Portuguese Malacca continued to attract a considerable portion of it. But the port was no longer the only trading center of any importance in the Straits, and, more significantly for the Malay world, its wealth no longer supported a court and a ruler who could trace his ancestry to the court of Srivijaya. As the trade had been splintered by the capture of Malacca, so political power in the Straits had become split between Aceh, which was fast becoming the most powerful Malay polity, and Johor, which, though weaker, still boasted a court ruled by the true Malaccan line, a potent factor in Malay politics. The conditions that had centered trade on Malacca had been destroyed, and merchant and prince alike had to settle for a less perfect world.

1. Tomé Pires, *Suma Oriental*, 228, quoted in Meilink-Roelofsz, *Asian Trade and European Influence between 1500 and about 1630*, 338. I have drawn heavily on Professor Meilink-Roeolfsz's description of Malay Malacca and its trade.

2. O. W. Wolters, *Early Indonesian Commerce*, 102, 127.

3. See O. W. Wolters, *The Fall of Srivijaya in Malay History*, 8–18, to understand the importance of Srivijaya in the Malay concept of themselves.

4. Ibid. 143ff.

5. M. A. P. Meilink-Roelofsz, *Asian Trade*, 43, [from Pires, *Suma Oriental*].

6. Wolters, *The Fall of Srivijaya*, 161. Wake, C. H, "Malacca's Early Kings and the Reception of Islam," *JSEAH* 5.2 (1964): 122.

7. Meilink-Roelofsz, *Asian Trade*, 60ff.

8. João de Barros, *Decadas* 2.6, [quoted in J. Crawfurd, *A Descriptive Dictionary of the Indian Islands and Adjacent Countries*, 245.]

9. Bailey W. Diffie and George D. Winius, *Foundations of the Portuguese Empire, 1415–1580*, 256. "The capture of Asia's greatest trading city by a mere 900 Portuguese and 200 Indians must rank as an event in the history of European expansion no less stunning than the better known conquest of Tenochtitlan by Hernando Cortés."

10. Ibid. 259. It was previously believed that they had more effective armaments, but this was not necessarily so. They had fewer artillery pieces than the Malays. Winius suggests that the Portuguese owed their success more to "superior tenacity and co-ordination" than to technological advantage.

11. Wolters, *The Fall of Srivijaya*, 176.

12. Ibid. And see A. C. Milner, *KERAJAAN; Malay Political Culture on the Eve of Colonial Rule*.

13. D. G. E. Hall, *A History of Southeast Asia*, 241.

14. Bailey and Winius, 320–21. "Each year they sent out armadas northward and southward from Goa between May and September—the season when the monsoons allowed coastal sailing. Those fleets obliged all private merchantmen plying the coast, Portuguese or native, to purchase Portuguese *cartazes*, or passes, themselves of negligible price. The real object of the *cartazes*, however, was not what they cost per se. but what a bearer was required to do as a consequence: to call in Portuguese ports."

I

THE DUTCH CONQUEST
OF MALACCA AND
ITS AFTERMATH

ON 14 JANUARY 1641, the forces of the United Netherlands East
Indies Company victoriously entered the Portuguese fortress of
Malacca. The news was received with jubilation at the Company's head-
quarters. "Thus falls into our hands this important fortress, generally
recognized as impregnable, with its cannon and all other war materials.
Henceforth it will be under the rule of the States General of the Free
United Netherlands, and his Royal Highness the Prince of Orange.
Further it will be considered private territory and a dominion of the
United Dutch East India Company."[1]

The United Dutch East India Company (Verenigde Oostindische
Compagnie, or VOC) had been set up in the Netherlands in 1602. It
incorporated the various smaller companies which had been sending
vessels to the East Indies, exploring the possibility of wresting the spice
trade from Portugal, to form a stronger and more capable whole. The
Netherlanders entered into the quest for the spice trade in the context
of their war to gain independence from Spain. Because of this, the new
United Company was designed to be a more effective weapon than the
separate provincial enterprises. This expectation was reflected in its
charter, which made the Company an armed and independent power in
Asia. It granted letters patent empowering the Company to act on
behalf of the Netherlands Government east of the Cape of Good Hope.

The VOC was able to wage war and conclude treaties in its own right with the powers of Asia. The charter also conferred on the VOC monopoly rights to all trade between the Netherlands and the East. A permanent capital of ƒ6,500,000 was provided, an amount almost ten times that available to its contemporary, the English East India Company. The Netherlands government did not reserve any rights to regulate or control the VOC's activities, which were left in charge of an authoritarian Board of Directors. Given the close structure of the Netherlands' ruling elite, members of the States General would automatically expect to have influence with the Directorate of the Company. The number of these directors gave rise to their popular name, the Heeren Zeventien, the Seventeen Gentlemen.[2]

The VOC hoped to establish immediately a strong base for its activities in the East, taking for its model the Portuguese, who had entered Asian trade a century before. Like the Portuguese, the Dutch aimed to capture a few strong ports and link them by their sea-power to support the factories set up in Asian courts. First choice naturally fell on Malacca, which had been the center of two empires, and was the base of their premier enemy in the East, the Portuguese. The Dutch launched an attack on Portuguese Malacca in 1606. They were assisted by the forces of the southern Malay state of Johor. This attempt failed, for the Portuguese had fortified the position strongly, and had beaten back many Malay attacks in the past ninety years of their occupation. Portuguese Malacca, though not as rich an entrepôt as its Malayan predecessor, was still in 1606 a force to be reckoned with. Further Dutch attempts on the town in 1608 and 1615 were equally unsuccessful. Malacca in Portuguese hands remained a stubborn enemy of advancing Dutch power, and a ready ally of the VOC's enemies, such as the Javanese Sultan Agung of Mataram.[3]

By 1609, the Company in Asia was beginning to assume the form which it was to keep for nearly two centuries. The Dutch Company was a hierarchy, ruled by a governor-general appointed by the Heeren Zeventien and charged with the selection of a council (the Council of the Indies) to help him govern the territories in the East. The governor-general in council in turn appointed governors and lesser officials to the growing number of out-stations—the *Buitencomptoiren,* permanent or semi-permanent factories or ports taken by force or negotiation from the local communities. Poor communications with the Netherlands meant that the governor-general was virtually independent in most of his decisions, and the power of his position varied only with the strength of the incumbent. In 1619, one of the strongest of these, Jan Coen, whose headquarters were at that time in the west Javanese principality of Bantam, captured Jacatra, a port on the northern coast of Java just east of the Sunda Straits. Renamed Batavia, this port became the center of VOC operations in Asia.

This move was to have long-term repercussions on the history of both Malacca and the VOC. Coen envisaged the VOC's network in Asia as a series of strong points connected by sea-power. Batavia was a practical alternative to Malacca as the headquarters of a company primarily interested in trade, for it commanded the Straits of Sunda, an important alternative route to the West, and occupied a central position in the Archipelago. The northern ports of Java had played an important role in the traditionally triangular spice trade, along with the Moluccas and Malacca.[4] The spice trade to the Moluccas had been dominated for centuries by merchants from northern Java, who had transported the spice-fruit to the Malay port for sale to international merchants from China, India, and further west. They had formed an integral part of a trade system revolving around Malacca. But Jacatra was too far south to command the Straits of Malacca, or, as time was to show, to serve as entrepôt to the tin, gold, and cloth trade of the Straits.

The establishment of Batavia did not, however, weaken the VOC's determination to take Malacca from the Portuguese. If anything, their efforts in this direction increased, for Malacca in Portuguese hands represented a serious threat to Batavia's trade. It dominated the main route from India to the East, along which flowed the VOC's trade from the Coromandel Coast (a most important section of the Company's trade in the early seventeenth century),[5] and hindered the VOC's participation in the useful tin and gold trade of the Malacca Straits, and the profitable sale of Indian cloth. The Portuguese claimed the right, as the overlords of Malacca, to monopolize this exchange. Above all it symbolized the survival of their main enemy in Asia, the Portuguese.

As the VOC grew in strength, it made new plans to drive the Portuguese from Malacca. Attempts made between 1623 and 1627 met with no success. In 1633 a blockade was set up, and approaches were made to the Malays of Aceh and Johor to ally with the Dutch forces. Aceh, the strongest Malay power, was reluctant to take part in this attack for several reasons—one of which was that it was still recovering from its own disastrous assault on the Portuguese in 1629. Though the VOC would patently have preferred an alliance with Aceh,[6] the southern state of Johor was less ambivalent, and thus it was the Johorese who assisted the Dutch in their final and victorious siege and assault on Malacca in 1640-41.[7]

After long years of fighting the Portuguese, the Dutch were naturally exultant at this victory. Governor-General Anthony van Dieman's letters to Europe were full of high hopes for the gains to be made from this new acquisition, which had not come cheap, having cost "a little under 1000 men killed in action and dead through epidemics,"[8] not to speak of the monetary outlay, (of which, of course, the Gentlemen spoke at length). "This victory has placed the Company in greater respect and security in these parts. Great trade will follow. All the neighbouring princes will respect us. ACHIN will remain our friend and probably grant us the 'toll' of the whole of Sumatra's west coast. MATARAM must befriend us, sell its rice in Batavia and buy its requirements from us."[9] As late as 1640 the specter of a Portuguese–Acehnese alliance had haunted the Governor-General and his Council, who had declared "It is in such cases that Malacca's strategic importance comes into bolder relief. THE CAPTURE OF MALACCA WILL EXCEL ALL THE CONQUESTS OF THE EAST INDIA COMPANY (DUTCH) IN INDIA."[10]

The immediate benefits were expected to be strategic. The VOC was at the time not on good terms with the powerful central Javanese power, Mataram. "We are confident that after the capture of Malacca this *restless guest* will himself ask for peace."[11] They believed the ruler of Mataram had aimed, by assisting Portuguese Malacca, to divert the VOC's attention from Java. Now Mataram was forced to look to Batavia instead of Malacca as the market for their most important export, rice.[12] Sultan Agung had to revoke his prohibition of the sale of rice to the Dutch.

The glamor of Malacca, which had so bewitched early Portuguese visitors, lingered still; the Dutch believed that "By capturing Malacca, the Portuguese monopolized the trade between East and West . . . making the city the chief centre of trade."[13] Malacca was expected to confer great material benefits on its new rulers. In 1638, the Governor-General had looked forward to the capture of the old fortress as a move in an overall strategic design to dominate the trade of the Archipelago. "It will be sufficient for us if we inherit the enemy's commerce, which must necessarily happen, and if we enjoy the fruits of the valuable trade in pepper, tin etc., which is to be driven in that area."[14] Though tarnished by the Portuguese occupation, Malacca's reputation still shone brightly in European eyes, and to the Dutch the port had remained the great trading center described by the first western visitors to the Indies.

With Malacca safely in Dutch hands, a reaction set in. There was disappointment about the amount of booty captured. The Dutch Company had hoped for substantial loot when the city finally fell, but it yielded only a surplus of about ƒ100,000.[15] The state of the town after it had been captured was very poor indeed. Still, Commissioner Jan Schouten, sent to review the situation and set up an orderly government, remained optimistic about the intrinsic value of the port to the VOC. "Malacca will be transformed into a flourishing place as soon as it gets its breath and resumes its normal position."[16]

But what was Malacca's "normal position" to be, now that it was for the first time in two-and-a-half centuries not the center of an empire? How could its "normal position" under Portuguese rule, where it had been the center of their operations in southeast Asia, be continued in the VOC's scheme of things, with the Company's outposts autocratically ruled from Batavia? Commissioner Schouten was from the outset acutely aware of this dichotomy, though he tried to mask it in his comments on Malacca's future role in the VOC—perhaps for the benefit of the Gentlemen in Europe, who had just spent so much to capture the port. Thus his optimistic statement; "By the expansion of trade in Malacca, Batavia will hardly be affected at all, because the people living between these two places will make their voyage according to the monsoons and consequently the diversion of trade to MALACCA will hardly be felt. On the contrary trade in Batavia will henceforth prosper more on account of the Javanese and MALACCAN traders."[17] The VOC was a trading company, and all its activities had to be justified in terms of profit and loss, rather than glory. Spain had declined beyond the point where aggressive action could be justified in terms of the war of independence—Portugal had itself broken away from Spain's rule in 1640.

The expensive policies pursued by van Dieman and his colleagues were viewed by the Heeren Zeventien in terms of the Company's balance sheet, not its strategy. The Gentlemen were interested in profit, not empire. So it was natural that the commercial possibilities and the rich past history of Malacca be stressed at this time, to justify the expense of the blockade.

Schouten's arguments are not convincing in view of Batavia's obvious fear of Malacca's competition. It is most unlikely that the government in Batavia really expected or desired Malacca's prosperity to revive in its new role as a subordinate port. On the other hand, they required that it revive enough to pay its way. The following years were to show Batavia working against Malacca's revival as an Archipelago or Asia-wide entrepôt in every way, in an attempt to re-direct Malacca's trade to the Javanese port, an attempt which was at best very partially successful. The only trade encouraged at Malacca was the local Straits trade, a trade Batavia seemed to misunderstand completely. From their writings both before and after the capture of Malacca, the VOC administration appeared to believe that the ruler of Malacca had some legal right to monopolize the local trade in tin, pepper, gold, and cloth. On the contrary, this trade had been attracted to Malacca because of its other successes. But the Dutch were to learn this fact of Malayan trade the hard way. One more element had been added to the forces splintering the trade of the Straits, and consequently splintering its political cohesion.

The commercial policies laid down by Batavia for the new Malaccan government were far from the open-handed encouragement of trade pursued by the Malay rulers. The Chinese trade presents us with an outstanding example of the restrictive policies applied to Malacca under Batavian rule. This trade, the original mainstay of the growth of Malacca as a major trading center, was discouraged and finally banned in 1654 by the Dutch. Chinese trade was a strong magnet which attracted vessels from all over the Archipelago and beyond. Company officials, recognizing this, soon tried to direct all the Chinese junks sailing south to Batavia.[18] The Chinese tried to continue their old established route to Malacca, for the journey to Batavia was longer. Many forsook Dutch ports altogether because of their harsh commercial policies and high tolls. It was well known even in later years that the Chinese junks which went to Johor, where they conducted their trade under circumstances far from ideal, would gladly have gone to Malacca instead if they could have been sure of acquiring the cargos they sought, especially pepper. But this would have been contrary to the *groet oogmerck* [grand design] of Batavia to attract all the Chinese trade to the Archipelago to itself, and the Council, it seems, preferred to lose this trade completely rather than have it go to Malacca.[19]

Malacca's trade was to be just as seriously curtailed in other areas. Despite his recommendation that "all means should be studied diligently to enlarge the trade of Malacca,"[20] Commissioner Schouten himself laid down a number of restrictions on commerce. The Company was to hold the monopoly in pepper, spices, opium, resin, sandalwood and tin, and also the principal lines in cloth and other profitable imported goods. These were to be exchanged at "reasonable prices," but it was soon clear that a price viewed as reasonable by the VOC authorities was often perceived as entirely unreasonable by the Malays. Restrictions were also placed on the availability of these items. Spices and pepper were only to be sold to merchants heading east to Manila, Macao, or the coast of China.[21] Heavy tolls were imposed on traders. Schouten outlined the export and import duties to be levied on vessels calling at Malacca in future.

The narrow attitude that profits could be made only when the Company controlled the buying and selling of a product—the "buy cheap, sell dear" policy expressed most fully in the VOC's conduct of the spice trade—was now also to be applied to the Malayan tin trade. On the purchase of Malayan tin, a useful item in the trade with India, Schouten envisaged a Dutch monopoly of the production of the Malay communities of Perak, Kedah, Ujung Salang [modern day Phuket], Bangkeri, and the whole southwest coast of Malaya, though the Portuguese had dealt only with Perak. He observed also that "it would be a good thing if the Company's territory could be cleared of MOORS [Indian Muslim traders], GENTYOS [Indian Hindu traders] and PORTUGUESE, because not only would more tin be secured but also large quantities of cloth could be marketed."[22] These Indian merchants had traditionally played a major role in the export of tin to India and the import of cotton piece goods to the Straits. If Batavia was to have its way, Malacca would be shorn of both the Chinese and Indian trade, the twin pillars on which all its past prosperity had stood.

It is not surprising that there were soon clear indications all was not well, and that Malacca was not the El Dorado the Batavian government claimed to have been anticipating. The expected profits were slow in coming. A summary of the VOC's entry into the Malaccan tin trade will serve to illustrate its difficulties. The Malaccan officers had been instructed to take over the Malayan tin trade, as tin was a useful article to send to the Coromandel. The Dutch and their European competitors had a fundamental problem in their trade with Asia. They were able to bring from their own lands little or nothing which was acceptable in exchange for the pepper and spices which had drawn them halfway round the world. They could use specie—silver and gold—but the export of these precious metals in any quantity was severely discouraged by their own governments. Spain solved the problem by plundering the New World, but this solution was not open to the Dutch. However, driven by their need, they soon discovered that sufficient profit could be made from trade within Asia to obtain capital to finance their purchases for Europe. This led to the VOC's involvement in the cloth trade of the Coromandel and its eagerness to dominate the tin trade.

This Dutch move into Malay trade coincided with a strong attempt on their part to reduce Asian competition in the valuable Coromandel cloth trade by exploiting the Company's control of the sea routes. To this end, passes were no longer issued freely to Indian shipping for destinations in the Straits of Malacca, and after 1641 were only issued for voyages to Malacca. Ships sailing to Malacca from Coromandel were to pay the same tolls they had formerly paid to the Portuguese. After 1647 even passes to Malacca were not issued, and Indian merchants sailing to the Straits risked seizure by VOC patrols. The Company was trying to eliminate totally their major competition, Indian merchants, in trade to the Straits.

They soon found that coercion of such a powerful group was impossible. This policy caused so much hostility on the Coromandel Coast that it endangered their whole situation there. Moreover, though the VOC's fleet was powerful in Asian terms, it was not equipped to police such stringent prohibitions, especially when, as was the case here, there were flouted by all the wealthier Indian merchants. The restrictions against Indian trade to the Straits were of necessity relaxed in the early 1650s.[23]

But the VOC had not abandoned its policy of winning over the profitable tin and cloth trade of the Malay regions. Having failed to control the Indian merchants, the Dutch now attempted to control the trade from the Malacca end. Monopoly contracts were negotiated between the Company and the rulers of various Malay ports, with the aim of channeling all the sale of cloth and purchase of tin to the VOC. Success in this venture seemed assured after the conquest of Malacca, for the Dutch believed that they had fallen heir to legal rights to a monopoly of trade in the area, which had been enjoyed previously by the Malays and the Portuguese.

The Dutch conquest of Malacca had indeed mightily impressed the Malay rulers, for the fortress still had an almost mystical significance for the Malay community. Moreover, the rulers were eager to explore any possibility of extricating themselves from their reliance on the Indian merchants, who totally controlled their most profitable export. So they were quick to welcome these powerful new customers, who seemed to promise relief from the economic stranglehold in which the Malays currently found themselves, and the Dutch were encouraged by the ease with which they obtained the promise of an exclusive tin trade in many Malay courts.

There had been a market for large quantities of Indian cloth in the Straits long before Malacca existed. Indian merchants had attained a crucial place in the tin trade, setting up agencies in the courts of the Malay rulers—for the tin often took months to collect in transportable quantities—advancing capital to them, all of whom were by 1641 deeply in debt to the Indian community.[24] The Sultan of Kedah quickly showed interest in an agreement with the Dutch, expressing himself willing to expel the Indian trading communities in return for Dutch protection. In 1642 he entered into a contract promising the VOC half of all the tin mined in or delivered to his country, for the fixed price of 31.25 rds per bahar. In 1643 the VOC obtained the right to trade at Ujung Salang, and in 1645 they contracted for the entire tin production of Bangkeri, to the north of Kedah. But significantly, the main tin-producing state of the Peninsula, Perak, which at that time paid allegiance to the court of Aceh, showed less enthusiasm for trade with the Dutch, who had to rely on their influence in Aceh to gain access to this vital source of supply.

Only too soon the Malay rulers came to realize that far from offering a profitable alternative to trade with the Indian merchants, the VOC was attempting to monopolize the traffic and paying unrealistically low prices into the bargain. Indian merchants enjoyed a freer trading structure than the agents of the Company, and could offer cloth at lower prices, and give higher prices in return for tin. Malay enthusiasm for doing business with the new power in the Peninsula quickly waned. Unfortunately the VOC and the Malay operated under entirely different preconceptions of the purposes of commercial agreements and the manner in which the tin trade was best operated. The Company saw their relations with the Malays not as purely commercial dealings, in which both sides should make a reasonable profit, but as a species of tribute trade to Malacca, not realizing that without a prestigious ruler of the old line, Malacca had no claim on the surrounding territories. The euphoria among VOC officials resulting from the victory in Malacca lasted until 1647—then the admission had to be made that the port was not doing well under Dutch rule. There had been no profit since 1641. No tin was being received from Kedah and Perak. Batavia, without considering the adoption of a more liberal commercial policy, decreed more forceful methods. It decided to ban totally all Indian trade to the Malay area. To enforce this, the Dutch imposed a naval blockade of the Straits. Armed Company vessels patrolled the vicinity of Malay ports and intercepted incoming vessels, which were allowed to proceed only if they were in possession of a pass issued by the relevant VOC authorities. The only vessels that were allowed to bypass Malacca without molestation, even if they did not have a pass, were those of Johor, the Company's ally in 1641, en route to Bengkalis, Siak, Kampar, and Rokan. The system had probably not changed much by the 1680s, when it was described irately by the Englishman, William Dampier:

> For where there is any Trade to be had, yet not sufficient to maintain a Factory; for where there may not be a convenient Place to build a fort, so as to secure the whole trade to themselves, they send their Guardships which, lying at the mouths of the Rivers, deter strangers from coming thither, and keep the petty Princes in awe of them. They commonly make a Shew as if they did this out of Kindness to the people; yet most of them know otherwise, but dare not openly resent it.[25]

These arrogant methods, borrowed largely from the Portuguese, met

with some immediate success, garnering significantly increased tin col-
lections until 1650. Malacca's finances improved markedly.²⁶ But any
Dutch hopes of permanently dominating the Malay tin trade were soon
shattered, as the Malay communities one after the other rebelled against
these aggressive tactics. In April, 1651, the twenty-seven Dutchmen
who manned the outpost at Perak were killed, and the lodge there
destroyed. Perak had never willingly agreed to break off trade with the
Indian merchants and deliver its tin to the VOC; it was only after the
intervention of its overlord, Aceh, that the Dutch gained entry to this
important source of the metal. An agreement was reached with the
Queen of Aceh that the VOC would receive half of the tin production
of Aceh's client state, Perak. In 1644–46 and 1647–49 Dutch vessels had
patrolled the Perak coast to force its inhabitants to deliver their tin to the
VOC. Resentment of Dutch methods and fear that the Dutch were plan-
ning to construct an armed fort in Perak finally provoked the violent
reaction of 1651. Despite many forceful protests by the Malacca government to the Sultans of Perak and Aceh, the main instigators of this act
were never punished.²⁷ In 1657 a blockade of Aceh and Perak was
mounted, nominally to force retribution for the murders of the Dutch in
Perak, but actually "to compel Aatchin, by depriving it of the extensive
importation of Moorish [Indian] cloth, to buy from the Honourable
Company."²⁸ Though Aceh was in 1659 forced to submit to VOC
demands, the Company's real aims were not met, for the blockade only
caused Indian shipping to go to other ports, and brought increased trade
with the English, who could not be excluded unless the Dutch were willing to risk strained relations in Europe. Meanwhile, Malacca's relations
with the other Malay communities deteriorated. In 1652 a Dutch envoy
was seized in Kedah, and again, the VOC could not obtain any redress.
And in April, 1658 , the factory and the patrol boat in Ujung Salang were
seized by Malay forces angered by the Dutch refusal to allow them to
trade in tin, and insistence on their right to search the Malay vessels. The
Dutch factory in Ujung Salang was withdrawn in 1660.

The VOC's prestige in the Straits was severely damaged by its inability to avenge these attacks, and the lesson was quickly learned by the
Malays that the Dutch were largely unable to enforce their grandiose
claims to monopoly.²⁹ Writing about the Ujung Salang incident in 1677
Governor Bort noted that:

Up to the present not the smallest vengeance has been taken nor punishment inflicted for this great murder and damage, nor has any satisfaction been given, wherefore the governors in that state have been encouraged and have become more insolent and petulant and have treated our people with so much less esteem and regard. They have even taken the whole of the trade from us and handed it over to other foreigners coming from abroad (contrary to old contracts made with the Honourable Company).[30]

Bort was incensed at the continuing trade of Ujung Salang with Indian, Javanese and other foreign merchants, who exported 600 bahar of tin from the island annually "without any regard to Malacca, [although] its dominion and jurisdiction in this strait have always extended to said island . . ."[31] Dutch Malacca's relations with all the Malay states had deteriorated considerably by 1660, and her trade was at a standstill.

Meanwhile, as the VOC spread out and took control of more areas of the Archipelago, Malacca lost its initial significance to the Dutch. Outside the Archipelago, the VOC had firmly established itself as a trading force throughout Asia; it had even secured a foothold in Japan, where no other foreign traders were admitted after 1641. Within the Archipelago, its increasing attempts to exclude other European traders were meeting with considerable success. In 1623 the "Amboina massacre" of the English had taken place in the Moluccas, and since then the Dutch had had no major competition for the spice trade. European merchants, however, still had access to spices brought to independent archipelagan ports. Even this situation was intolerable to the VOC. Macassar, in the east of the Archipelago, remained a haven for foreign traders, both European and Asian; in 1667 this port was also brought under VOC control. By the late 1660s Bantam in east Java remained the only major port open to Europeans other than the Dutch, and in 1684 it too fell into the Dutch sphere of influence. The second half of the seventeenth century saw great territorial expansion and great change come to the VOC, as it struggled to become a force in the vigorous world of inter-Asian commerce. In the 1650s trade was still emphasized as the Company's main purpose, but during the next three decades the nature of the VOC was to change, as the internal affairs of Mataram and Bantam drew the VOC into territorial interests not previously contemplated, and the need to maintain strong garrisons at Bantam and

Macassar, as well as Malacca, put more emphasis on the Company's growing role as a territorial power.

In the Straits area itself, by 1662 the VOC achieved a peaceful coup in west Sumatra that promised to keep the Company supplied with the highly prized pepper crop of the Sumatran highlands. This coup also reduced the power of Aceh by diminishing its attraction as an entrepôt and its wealth. But Aceh's decline was not reflected in any increase in Malacca's trade. None of the efforts of the 1650s had succeeded in restoring a profitable trade to the old port. As it became increasingly clear that occupation of the fortress Malacca carried with it no automatic right to control the tin and cloth trade of the Straits, the Heeren Zeventien began to reconsider this "profitless" and expensive settlement, with an eye, ever present in their case, to cutting costs. The post was reduced in status in 1662, when Jan van Riebeeck was appointed to head the government there with the rank of commander, not governor. There was for a time even discussion of evacuating the port. Was Malacca, captured with such jubilation and high hopes, to be abandoned by the Dutch after a mere twenty-one years of occupation?

In the end no such drastic measures were taken; withdrawal from Malacca would surely have diminished the VOC in the eyes of the Malays and other archipelagan peoples, and Malacca was after all situated on a strategically vital waterway and could not be allowed to fall into the hands of the Company's competitors. Jan van Reibeeck's successor, Balthasar Bort, and all subsequent rulers of Malacca were restored to the rank of governor. Trade revived somewhat during Bort's term of office, the improvement being due to both his intimate knowledge of the area and skill in dealing with the Malays, and the timely discovery of tin deposits on the Siak river in 1674. But for Malacca, the days of prestige and glamor were over. By 1678 Malacca's main function was to act as a provisioning port for the passing trade, which would still appear to have been voluminous. Bort lists in detail the places to the north, northeast, and south from which ships or smaller vessels passed through the Straits, commenting that:

> This traffic of course occasions trade among the people in food, clothing and other necessities, but little in merchandise, since the Company's and most native ships come here only to provide themselves with necessaries and then proceed to other places with their cargo (without unloading it

here), except those whose custom it is (that is Company's ships) to bring to Malacca what is requisitioned . . .[32]

Malacca's place in VOC hierarchy had by the 1670s been thoroughly defined. It was a provisioning port of too much strategic importance to be abandoned, but of too little independent commercial value to challenge Batavia's new role as the "queen of the east."

Several themes begin to recur in the correspondence between the Malacca government and its masters in Batavia. How will Malacca pay its costs? How was the Company to compete with the many successful Asian merchants, from India and the Peninsula, who had scant respect for the Company's rules and regulations? The Malay rulers had realized just how few resources the Dutch Company was prepared to allocate to its outpost in the Straits, and flouted it wherever they could. Note was already being taken in Malacca of visits by English and other European merchants to neighboring ports in search of tin and pepper.[33] The trade of the Indians had by this time been accepted by the Dutch as a necessary evil. It was reckoned better to receive them at Malacca and at least collect their port dues, than to have them visit the Malay ports. Even if they could have been excluded from the Straits altogether, it was now admitted, the result would only have been that the English and Danes would have come in their place. As it was Europeans were increasingly involved in the Manila[34] and the tin trades. Tin was the major article of merchandise purchased for the Company in the Straits, but in the 1660s the Malaccan authorities had increasing difficulties in maintaining supplies. Patrols at the mouth of the Perak and Kedah Rivers did not much help. Even the new trade with Patupahan on the Siak River, which Bort had begun in 1676, was by the time he left Malacca two years later being menaced by Johor, which claimed suzerainty and prior rights to the area.

The growing friction between Malacca and Johor over the Siak trade in the later 1670s underlines a significant change in Malay politics since the Dutch capture of Malacca. Johor, the VOC's ally in that venture, had flourished in the decades since 1640. Despite some disagreements with the Dutch in the early years of their new government, the southern Malay state had profited immensely from its decision to throw in its lot with the VOC. The Sultan and *orang kaya* of Johor were allowed to trade to Malacca toll-free, and made the most of this dispensation.

Moreover, the power of Aceh, which had kept Johor in check for a century, had begun to wane when the Dutch established themselves in the Straits. Some of Aceh's problems, such as the rise to power of an elite which fought to keep the central authority weak, and the revolt of the valuable pepper provinces of the west coast, were, strictly speaking, internal matters. But the west coast dependencies were only able to break their ties with Aceh proper because they had attached themselves to the VOC, which provided them with both a market and protection. By the 1660s Aceh no longer posed a threat Johor, and the southern state had begun to expand its own operations. A war with Jambi interrupted Johor's growing prosperity for a time, but the policies of the powerful Johor ruler, the Paduka Raja Abd al-Jamil, began to pay off in earnest in the late 1670s.[35]

From this time on Malaccan officials and other sources report a heavy international trade at the new Johorese capital of Riau, on the island of Bintan immediately south of Singapore. This trade must have been greatly increased when in 1684 the VOC took over Bantam in northwest Java, the last established independent port in the Archipelago open to foreign trade. In 1687 an envoy from Malacca reported five to six hundred boats in the Riau River. There were six large ships from Siam, three large Chinese vessels, two vessels from Palembang with cargos of pepper, Portuguese ships from Manila, English ships, and, of course, numerous vessels from Johor's dependencies in the Peninsula and eastern Sumatra, and from Aceh, Perak, Kedah, and Siantan were attracted to the new entrepôt, where tin, pepper, Indian cotton goods, and other wares which had been traditionally available at Malacca could be obtained without the difficulty and high tolls now imposed at that port by the Dutch government.[36] Malacca was jealous of this growing prosperity, and felt Johor posed a threat to its own trade. Batavia sent a mission to Riau to negotiate a treaty in 1685, but Raja Abd al-Jamil, secure in his power and knowing how much it was based on this trade, respectfully refused to make concessions. He did however sign a treaty of friendship with the VOC and reiterated the hope that the Dutch and Johor would always remain the good friends and allies they had been in the past. Some confusion arose at this point, and spilled over into later historical accounts of VOC-Johor relations, because two versions of this treaty were drawn up; the one in Malay, which was the treaty to which

Abd al-Jamil had actually agreed, and another in Dutch, which incorporated many commercial concessions not listed in the Malay version. The Company's lack of a competent translator would seem to have caused this misunderstanding. The Paduka Raja did not, however, leave the Company in any doubt as to his repudiation of this questionable Dutch document, once he was aware of its existence. The Batavian Government preferred not to attempt to force the issue at this time; they were already embroiled in a war in Java, and wished to keep the peace with Johor, which after all shared their need to keep the Malacca Straits peaceful and open to international shipping.[37]

Still, the friction continued between Johor and Malacca, especially over the valuable Siak trade, and when the experienced Paduka Raja was ousted by a coup d'état in Johor in 1688, and the court removed to the Johor River, Malacca felt the time was ripe to try for new concessions. Envoys were sent to Johor in March, 1689. Surprisingly, this mission was marked with great apparent success; large concessions were granted to the VOC, covering most of what had been required in 1685. The experiences of the next decade, however, proved that the concessions had been illusory. Johor and its trade continued to flourish, while protesting always its great friendship with the Dutch Company. Johor's new leaders had in 1689 merely used the new Dutch "alliance" to strengthen their own internal position, and then proceeded to use various loopholes, including their knowledge of the conflict of interest between Batavia and Malacca in the matter of the Straits trade, to protect their own activities from serious Dutch retribution. Trade at Johor under the new regime flourished; so much so that by 1697 "there was no doubt that Johor was the pre-eminent military and economic power of the Malay world."[38]

By the end of the seventeenth century, it was abundantly clear that Malacca's role in the commercial empire of the VOC was to be substantially different from that which it had played when under Portuguese or Malay rule. The VOC was established as a great power in the Archipelago, and was well on the way to becoming an important territorial power in Java. Its lifeline to Europe had been set up through the Sunda Straits and west rather than north through the Straits of Malacca; even the trade to the Coromandel Coast, which had earlier made this route vitally important, had declined by the beginning of the eighteenth century. Batavia was now the "queen of the east" to which the international trade was to be drawn. The VOC retained Malacca not for its own sake, as the Portuguese had done, but as a strategic outpost, a ghost of its former self which could not even dominate the second-rate local powers of the Malacca Straits and gather to itself the profits of the tin trade.

This left the door open for a Malay power to regain the wealth and position which had previously been the prerequisite of the dominant port of the Straits of Malacca, and the VOC's central government showed no great signs of resisting the emergence of such a power. Batavia's attitude to the Malay kingdom which Malacca regarded as its chief rival and the block in its road to economic security was conciliatory, not confrontational. Batavia had little will to add Johor to its list of conquests, for the rewards would be small, the costs large; moreover, the VOC itself benefited from Johor's strength. Johor was now both motivated and able to police the Straits and keep them free of piracy and minor warfare, a freedom, at someone else's expense, which Batavia appreciated. At times Johor seemed to be more in favor with Batavia than Malacca. At the turn of the eighteenth century, the chief role of Malacca was to forestall any other European settlement in Straits, and to cost the VOC as little as possible in the process. Except for that, and the maintenance of its alliance with Johor, Jan Compagnie seemed to have largely withdrawn its interest from the Straits of Malacca—even from tin-rich Perak.

NOTES

1. P. A. Leupe, "The Siege and Capture of Malacca from the Portuguese in 1640–1641," *JMBRAS*, 14.1 (1936): 47.

2. K. Glamann, *Dutch-Asiatic Trade, 1620–1740*, 4–5.

3. D. G. E. Hall, *History of South East Asia*, 317.

4. Meilink-Roelofsz, *Asian Trade*, 103.

5. T. Raychaudhuri, *Jan Company in Coromandel 1605–1690*, 159.

6. Leupe, 15, 17 and 18.

7. D. K. Bassett, "Changes in the Pattern of Malay Politics, 1629–1655," *JSEAH* 10.3 (1969): 435.

8. Leupe, 48.

9. Ibid. 49, (quoting Generale Missiven 31 January 1641.)

10. Ibid. 24.

11. Ibid. 18.

12. Hall, *History of South East Asia,* 318.

13. Leupe, 1.

14. Graham Irwin, "The Dutch and the Tin Trade of Malaya in the 17th century," in Jerome Ch'en and Nicholas Tarling, *Studies in the Social History of China and Southeast Asia; Essays in Memory of Victor Purcell,* 276.

15. Leupe, 61.

16. Ibid. 125.

17. Ibid. 140.

18. W. Ph. Coolhaas, *Generale Missiven van Gouverneurs-Generaal en Raaden aan Heren XVII der Verenigde Oostindische Compagnie,* vol. 2: 824.

19. Ibid. 5: 628, (6 December 1693).

20. Leupe, 140.

21. C. O. Blagden, "Report of Governor Balthasar Bort on Malacca," *JMBRAS* 5.1 (1927): 125.

22. Ibid. 142.

23. Raychaudhuri, *Jan Company in Coromandel,* 122–24.

24. Irwin, "The Dutch and Tin Trade," 272–73.

25. William Dampier, *Voyages and Discoveries,* 113.

26. Irwin, "The Dutch and Tin Trade," 280–81.

27. Barbara Andaya Watson, *Perak, the Abode of Grace,* 45–48.

28. Cited in Blagden, 132.

29. Irwin, "The Dutch and Tin Trade," 285.

30. Cited in Blagden, 162, 163.

31. Ibid.

32. Cited in Blagden, 130.

33. Blagden, 133ff.

34. The Manila trade involved the profitable sale of spices and pepper to Indian merchants trading to the Philippines via the Malacca Straits. They often served as a cover for European independent merchants, to circumvent Spanish regulations barring foreign Europeans from trade with Manila.

35. Leonard Y. Andaya, *The Kingdom of Johor 1641–1728,* 127ff.

36. Ibid. 148–49.

37. Ibid. 143–44.

38. Ibid. 181.

2

THE CRISIS WITH JOHOR,
1700–1718

THE DISPERSION of Malacca's trade, which had begun with the capture of the port by the Portuguese, accelerated significantly after the Dutch East India Company's victory in 1641. Foreign merchants forsook the old entrepôt for numerous smaller Malay ports, of which Johor, at the southern tip of the Malay Peninsula, had by the late seventeenth century became the most prominent.[1] Given the Company's policy of repressing free trade in Malacca, at the turn of the eighteenth century it seemed likely that Johor would remain the port in the Straits most favored by the foreign merchants, and consequently the strongest power of the Malay world, no matter how stridently the Dutch government at Malacca protested. The VOC had shown no interest in extending its control in the Straits beyond the mere physical occupation of Malacca, and relied on the strength of its ally Johor to keep the area safe for Company shipping, which had dropped off now that the Coromandel trade had become a much less important sector of the Company's Asian trade.[2]

But this policy of combining occupation of Malacca and alliance with Johor ran into snags early in the eighteenth century, for Johor also had its problems. Rivalry between the families which traditionally filled the posts of Bendahara and Laksamana had led in 1688 to a coup d'état which removed the regent, the Paduka Raja Tun Abd al-Jamil, who had ruled in the name of the young sultan, Mahmud. The successful engineer of this coup, the Bendahara Tun Habib Abd al-Majid, managed to maintain Johor's prosperity almost uninterrupted, though he made paper concessions to Malacca in 1689. However, his control of Johor hinged largely on his control of Mahmud, the last remaining member of the old Malacca line, whose prestige as ruler did much to ensure Johor's predominance in the Malay world. Sultan Mahmud, kidnapped at an early age, grew into an extremely disturbed youth, sadistic and irresponsible.[3] When the old Bendahara died in 1697, his son Tun Abd al-Jalil, who succeeded him in the post, was unable to control the young ruler. The resulting disorder in Johor brought about by this division in government caused Johor's trade, which depended as surely as had Malay Malacca's on the wise and energetic policies of its rulers, to disintegrate. "In just two years Johor had changed from the acknowledged leading entrepôt of the Malay world to a small backwater port."[4] The *orang kaya* of Johor were faced not only with the personal provocations of the irrational behavior of the Sultan, but also the prospect that this same behavior would totally ruin Johor's prosperity. In 1699 one or both of these provocations drove a member of the court to murder the young Sultan. As there was no possible heir of the blood, the Bendahara Abd al-Jalil, the legal heir in such a case, was declared Sultan by the other *orang kaya*.

Though this desperate act restored some peace to the court itself, it had the immediate and critical effect of severely weakening Johor in relation to the other Malay communities of the Straits of Malacca. Taking an extreme example, the rulers of Perak and Palembang, who had links with the old Malacca family, threatened retaliation, and many of the smaller communities undoubtedly felt that their obligations to Johor had been broken. Johor's internal structure was also weakened, since, as Leonard Andaya argues, the *daulat* of the Malacca line was no longer present to hold the community together.[5] But the damage did not cause immediate disintegration, and under the able leadership of the new Bendahara, Sultan Abd al-Jalil's brother, Johor was able to resume its role as major host to the passing trade.

Malacca did not profit from Johor's problems any more than it had from Aceh's. At the beginning of the eighteenth century the English merchant-captain Charles Lockyer visited the port of Malacca; later he recalled it as "a healthful place, but of no great trade."[6] The Malacca government had many complaints of Johor's "illegal" rivalry for the local trade, and in 1705 Governor Carol Bolnar, acting on his own initiative, sent an envoy to Johor to complain about the various infringements of the VOC's rights.[7] The Malaccan Governor may have felt that the time was ripe to reshape the relationship with Johor, while the new sultanate was struggling to establish itself on both the domestic and international levels. Whatever weaknesses plagued Johor's new rulers, they still appear to have felt perfectly safe in rejecting Malacca's demands, secure in the knowledge that they had no quarrel with Batavia. They were justified in this opinion; the Malaccan mission, made without the Governor-General's consent, was doomed from the start, and was swiftly nullified by a conciliatory embassy from Batavia to Johor in 1706. Obviously, at that date the Governor-General did not feel that Johor's rivalry with Malacca was encroaching on the VOC's preserves in any serious way.

However, the dilemmas facing Johor's new dynasty were to have further effects on VOC-Johor relations despite the attempts of the Batavian government to retain the old status. The Bendahara sultanate was beset with a variety of problems, not least the loss of the *daulat* of the old Malacca line on the death of Mahmud. This mythical, almost metaphysical force played a highly important role in keeping a Malay state's scattered population under control. In the period 1699–1707, the new Bendahara, an elder brother of the new Sultan who had taken over this post and the administration of Johor in 1699, had faced many challenges to the regime.[8] In 1708 he died, and the Sultan's younger brother, the Raja Muda Mahmud, already known in Malacca as a powerful force in the court, took formal control of his family's, and Johor's, fortunes. The Raja Muda obviously believed that more positive measures were called for to set his family firmly in power, for under his rule Johor embarked on an aggressive policy of expansion which was to bring it into conflict with the VOC much more directly than ever before, even under the Paduka Raja Tun Abd al-Jamil in the 1670s.[9]

The Raja Muda removed the court immediately to Riau, on the island of Bintan; this was a bold step, signaling a new approach to the commercial scene, or rather, a return to an approach that had been overwhelmingly successful thirty years earlier when Johor first emerged as the major commercial power of the Straits. Riau had then been the chosen capital of the Paduka Raja Tun Abd al-Jamil.[10] After his overthrow, the court had returned to the safety of the Johor River on the mainland. But the island of Bintan was the ideal location for an entrepôt, centrally situated to all the trade routes which converged on the Straits, and in the heartland of the *orang laut,* the sea-going clan which had been the traditional mainstay of the sultans of Johor. Governor Pieter Rooselaar of Malacca noted that Riau was in a most advantageous position to attract trade, close to the routes of the Chinese junks in their annual voyages, and of ships coming to and from Thailand [Siam] and Kampuchea [Cambodia].[11] In the context of Malay history, this move signified expansion. It may have been the courage of desperation, an attempt to secure the new dynasty by taking a high hand. Whatever the motives which decided the Raja Muda on this move, it signified trouble for Malacca.

The Raja Muda swiftly stepped up the pressure on the outer territories to deliver all their products to Johor, a policy which threatened, among other things, to cut off Malacca's lucrative trade with Siak. In 1710, Malacca reported that envoys had come from the Raja Muda of Johor with the "sharp and unreasonable request" that no more ships belonging either to the VOC or the Malacca freeburghers[12] be sent to trade at Bengkalis, the port on the Siak River, or into the Siak River itself.[13] The Malacca officials were highly incensed, claiming in their next letter to Batavia that the Malacca freeburghers had "always" gone to the Siak River toll-free and without any restrictions (the trade actually dated back only to the 1680s.) Siak trade had become a very critical matter to the Malaccan authorities, for both the revenues of the port and the private incomes of the VOC authorities had by now come to depend very heavily upon it.[14] The connection had been forged after the discovery of tin in the Siak uplands in the 1670s, but the Siak river was also a valuable point of access to the inland Minangkabau Empire, and supported a trade in tin, pepper, cloth, and gold of considerable importance. It might not have been coincidental that this trade opened up to Malacca (or Johor, depending on which of the two could command it) after the Dutch agreements with the rulers on the west coast of Sumatra cut Aceh off from this area. Not long after the VOC negotiated their treaties with the west coast, the English trader William Dampier noted that the folk of Bengkalis, the port at the mouth of the Siak river, seemed wholly dependent on their trade with the Dutch.[15] Alexander Hamilton, trading in the Straits in the first decade of the eighteen century, observed that the Dutch had a factory on the side of a large river "called *Benkalis*," where the Company sold a great deal of cloth and opium and bought gold dust in return. Judging from the complaints of the Malaccan authorities about the state of trade this was an overestimation; there is a reference in a letter from Batavia to Europe in 1695 to a post at Siak which was not very lucrative and would probably be disbanded.[16] But Siak was important to Malacca. A profitable trade was being driven at Bengkalis by the freeburghers of Malacca, and revenue from tolls and duties paid on this trade now made up a good portion of Malacca's income.

Conflict over this trade to Sumatra had already driven a wedge between Malacca and Johor in the 1680s. Now it was feared in Malacca that these moves by Johor, especially the attempted closure of the Siak trade, would ruin the domestic trade, one of the port's few sources of income. Batavia, hoping to call the Raja Muda's bluff, counselled Malacca to ignore this move on Johor's part and continue to grant passes to the disputed area.[17] But Mahmud was not bluffing, as he proceeded to demonstrate. Malaccan merchants who continued to trade to Bengkalis and the Siak River were charged 10 percent duty, and some even had their ships and cargos seized by Johor officials[18] The Malacca government accused Johor of trying to ruin its merchants. It feared that many of the freeburghers would abandon Malacca if their trade continued to be threatened in this way. Such a loss would have been a major blow to Malacca's domestic finances.[19] The Raja Muda remained adamant. He had, he declared in a letter to the Malacca government in 1711, no wish to disturb the long standing friendship between his country and the VOC, but he pointed out that the agreement allowing the VOC to trade to Johor's territory of Siak had never included the freeburghers, and that the VOC itself had not conducted any business there for several years. "His Majesty [Sultan Abd al-Jalil], I, and my council, have . . . resolved and approved that the trade of Siacca [Siak] from the time that the Company abandoned the place reverted solely to us."[20] He had, he explained, decided to place restrictions on the trade to curb the interloping of the Malaccan freeburghers. His aim was surely to force as much of the produce of this valuable tin and gold producing area, and the trade which came down the river from the Minangkabau lands of the west coast, to his own entrepôt at Riau. He was again following in the footsteps of Tun Abd al-Jamil, though he was showing a willingness to antagonize the VOC unusual in a Johor ruler. Johor officials in Siak continued to harass the Malacca freeburghers.

Throughout 1711 and 1712 Johor also forcibly diverted to Riau such Chinese junks as still sailed annually to Malacca, and even Javanese vessels which supplied the VOC town with provisions. The Governor-General reported that the Raja Muda had become "so assured, as to proclaim in the name of the King of Johoor that no Javanese vessels were to go to Malacca, but were to come instead to Johoor."[21] This trade largely involved the cartage of foodstuffs, principally rice and salt, and a little sugar and tobacco. Malacca was totally dependent on imported foodstuffs, and to maintain even its slender role as a provisioning port it relied on these imports, so this was another major threat to its economic survival.

In an attempt to resolve the prickly Siak issue, Malacca sent the envoys Jan Lispencier and Thimonus Molenaenus to Riau in January, 1713, with instructions to negotiate a treaty that would guarantee access to Siak and other Johor territories. They were equipped with a draft agreement intended to re-affirm the major concessions granted to the VOC by Johor in the defunct treaties of 1685 and 1689. This draft proposed that the "old alliance and friendship" be renewed; the Company was to be granted the right to freely enter all lands "which are at present (or may be in the future) ruled by [the Sultan of Johor]," and to trade there under fair conditions and tolls. In return, the Sultan and notables of Johor, and their dependents, would be entitled to trade on similar terms at Malacca (within the limits of the prohibitions imposed on the port by Batavia), except in opium. A special clause stipulated that the freeburghers of Malacca would be granted the same privileges as the Company, especially in the Siak River, and that within the territories of Johor they need not pay any tolls or be impeded in any way. The VOC and the freeburghers were to be allowed to obtain masts and other timbers for their vessels from the Siak River without let or hindrance. The draft also stipulated that in future, no acts of aggression were to be committed against the people of Malacca by the Johorese, and that if, notwithstanding, any such outrages were to occur, the perpetrators were to be appropriately punished.[22]

This draft makes clear Malacca's many grievances, but the envoys' instructions do not indicate just how such important concessions were to be wrung from an unsympathetic Johor. Simply to reiterate demands which had been evaded for seventy years would seem to have been a pointless exercise. Probably, Malacca officials, drawing on their predecessors' experience with Johor over the last century, believed that the Raja Muda would compromise when openly confronted by the displeasure of the Dutch and revert to the traditional Johor policy of public deference to the VOC. Then they could at least regain the pre-1708 position, when Johor, though a damaging rival to Malacca, had not been actively hostile. The few threats with which the envoys were equipped included the withdrawal of the right of Johor notables to free trade at Malacca (a right often bitterly resented by the Malacca officials and claimed to be much abused by the Johorese), the confiscation of a trading vessel and its cargo belonging to the Raja Muda which had been impounded by the VOC in Negapatnam, and the confiscation of a cargo of opium of which he owned part, held at Malacca.[23]

But Mahmud was not to be diverted from his course.[24] He kept the matter of Siak trade to the forefront, adding to his former justifications for his actions the new claim that Patupahan itself was a subject territory of Johor. This was now one of the main inland tin producing communities using the Siak River. The Dutch envoys protested that Patupahan had always been independent. The Raja Muda became offended by this claim, which he saw as a slight to Johor's prestige, and declared that the Malacca freeburghers would not be allowed to trade in Patupahan even if they were able to find an alternate route into the area.[25] The embassy returned empty-handed, and Johor continued to show scant respect for Malacca's local trade.

However, Malacca was not alone, it was a cog in the vast machinery of VOC trade. Though normally it suited the overall interests of this trade to encourage the existence of a strong Malay state in the Straits, even at the expense of Malacca's trade and its Governor's temper, such open competition as Mahmud was practicing was not good for the Company's image. The Batavian government chose to side with Malacca in this dispute. Batavia appears to have been incensed by Mahmud's actions, and regularly referred to him in hostile terms in their reports home at this time. This ruler,"despite all our civilities in his regard, has given the Hon. Compagnie much cause of resentment over his conduct, and for a long time has tried to draw off trade from Malacca to Riau."[26] Batavia certainly had no desire to contain the old port of Malacca merely to see the rise of a Malay entrepôt at Riau in its place.

To prove his support of Malacca, the Governor-General now sent two armed vessels, the *De Jordoon* and the *De Combarden,* to cruise in the vicinity of Riau.[27] An embassy was also sent to Johor to underline the concern felt by Batavia at the Raja Muda's activities. Johor had always been sensitive to where the real power lay in the VOC, and this move demonstrated to them that the Dutch displeasure must be taken seriously. Batavia's action certainly "gave the Johoorese some second thoughts,"[28] as the Governor-General later wrote. It did force the Raja Muda to make placatory moves towards the VOC; a mission soon arrived at Batavia from Johor to negotiate a new treaty, with letters from Sultan Abd al-Jalil and the Raja Muda expressing the hope that the VOC would continue Johor's friend and ally.[29] In striking contrast to their attitude towards the Malaccan embassy, the Johorese were anxious to conciliate the Batavian officials of the VOC, and a treaty which essentially yielded all the concessions Malacca had previously demanded was prepared and mutually agreed upon by 19 August 1713.[30] Malacca's worries would seem to have been at an end.[31]

But the tone of the VOC correspondence of the succeeding period belies this victory. The Raja Muda had played the old game of yielding the VOC everything in appearance but nothing in reality. Johor continued in all the objectionable practices which had given rise to the negotiations. Malacca's freeburghers were still being obstructed in their Siak trade.[32] The disruption increased when Johor launched an attack on Patupahan, and later Inderagiri. A large Johor fleet patrolled the Straits, diverting to Riau vessels bound for Malacca from Java's east coast and elsewhere. "This piratical people, with their plundering and murdering" were making Malacca's foreshores unsafe, "to the damage of the small native trader, and disrespect of the Compagnie." Malacca's trade was so badly affected in 1714 that the town suffered from a shortage of rice, for the grain usually brought from Java had been diverted to Riau. Malacca's freeburghers were forced to fetch grain from Riau.[34]

And the supposedly successful treaty, though apparently negotiated to the satisfaction of both parties in 1713, had not yet been ratified by Mahmud. The Raja Muda protested that he could not sign the form of the treaty sent to Riau for it was incorrect in Malay terms and highly disrespectful to himself.[35] The Malaccan Dutch felt this to be merely a pretext to delay the implementation of the treaty; Governor Moerman declared it a "frivolous" excuse not to ratify the document. Perhaps with some reason; for though the situation could have arisen from cultural misunderstandings, and Mahmud may indeed have been forced to delay against his own political interests the implementation of his alliance with the VOC, his continuing disregard for Malacca's goodwill bears out Moerman's opinion.[36] The Johor ruler's actions immediately after the conclusion of the 1713 treaty indicates that, like its forerunners of 1685 and 1689, this treaty was only a diplomatic sop thrown out by Johor to allay Batavia's hostility or, at least, to delay the consequences of it.

In 1713, Johor was a powerful and expanding force in the Straits, believing itself strong enough to challenge the Malacca government with impunity, but still cautious about confronting the main body of the VOC; though by 1714 even this consideration seemed not to weigh too heavily with Raja Muda Mahmud. Despite the treaty he had just signed, Mahmud's attempts to draw trade to Riau grew ever greater. Batavia learned that foreign merchants were buying spices at Riau at substantially lower prices than those offered by the Dutch (when they were allowed to sell this precious commodity).[37] The spices were being obtained clandestinely from VOC officials at Macassar who stood to gain hugely from this illicit trade.[38] Riau's trade in locally produced tin and pepper was also flourishing, as Chinese and other foreign merchants flocked there. In 1714, the Chinese alone exported 500,000 lbs tin and 2,500 piculs pepper.[39] Thanks to its uncompetitive prices Malacca was finding it impossible to acquire enough tin to satisfy the VOC's trading needs. Pepper seems to have been brought to Riau mainly from Palembang, in defiance of the Palembang Raja's treaties with the VOC. In 1714 Mahmud attempted to cement this connection by arranging a marriage alliance between his daughter and a Palembang prince, but in this he was unsuccessful.[40]

Relations with Johor continued to take a prominent place in the Malacca-Batavia correspondence throughout 1714. The seriousness with which Batavia took the problem cannot be doubted—Riau had far surpassed Malacca in the contest for the local trade, and could conceivably pose a threat to Batavia itself if allowed to continue unimpeded. The Malacca Governor was asked in 1714 for "some opinion on how to constrain Johoor." Batavia even questioned whether it would be better to push for an open rupture, and asked for details of the size of Johor's forces.[41] Malacca supplied a full description of Johor's strength, and their own; the Johorese could call on a total of 6500 soldiers and more than 233 vessels of all types, as opposed to Malacca's meagre garrison of less than 500.[42] Malacca could not hope to stand against Johor without substantial reinforcements from Batavia. Moreover, Governor Moerman believed it highly likely that the French, the English, or even the Portuguese would be quick to take advantage of any conflict in the Straits. If the VOC was to move at all it must move swiftly and in strength, and Batavia must supply this strength. This would require a major commitment of men and munitions.

But this was not the era of van Dieman or Speelman; the power of the Netherlands had been slowly eroded in the last couple of decades and now, at the end of a long and grueling European war (the War of Spanish Succession), the Heeren Zeventien would not view with favor anything which could provoke a new conflict. An important consideration was the likelihood that another European nation would intervene in such quarrel, either openly or clandestinely.[43] The VOC no longer possessed the power to close off the Malay world to other Europeans. Sixty years' experience in the Straits had shown that the VOC could not compete with private Asian or even private European merchants in this arena. Batavia's resources were already strained by a new war in Java and a campaign on the Malabar coast in India, both areas of far more significance in the overall trade-structure of the VOC than the Malacca Straits.[44] In June, 1715 the Batavian government informed Malacca that "our intention this year is not to undertake any action against Johoor," for after due consideration of the situation it had been decided "not to engage in a war of uncertain success." While promising that the VOC intended only to postpone Johor's punishment, the Governor-General counselled Governor Moerman to take care not to give the Raja Muda any cause of offense "for the time being."[45]

Throughout 1715 and 1716 Johor's fleets "continued to prey on Asian vessels in the seas around Malacca, not even respecting vessels of the inhabitants of Malacca which are supplied with official passes."[46] Raja Muda Mahmud continued to ignore the wishes of the Malacca government, such as the demand for reparation for the captured cargo of Pieter Domingos Jans, a Malacca resident. Governor Moerman was suspicious of Johor's intentions respecting Malacca, and the Malaccan Syahbandar, Anthony van Aldorp, was sent to Riau in late 1715 to collect information about the continuing spice trade and report on Johor's other activities. In 1716, Batavia wrote again that the VOC had "wished for a long time to bring this prince to reason," but that lack of sufficient supplies of men and equipment prevented such an undertaking at the present time. Malacca was again urged to maintain a "strict neutrality" in Malay affairs, so that the Company would not be drawn into "another untimely war.

The decision not to take any police action against Johor, though couched in terms which left open the possibility of revision, established Batavia's de facto policy towards the Straits of Malacca for the next five decades. This policy had grown up as a result of the VOC's experience in the area in the later part of the seventeenth century. Abandoning the forceful intervention which had won Malacca and contributed to the decline of Aceh after 1641, Batavia had maintained its alliance with the new dominant Malay power, Johor, despite the discontent of Malacca (though it had tried occasionally to bluff Johor into concessions), because it saw that a strong Johor would help maintain order in the vital sea lane, removing some of the burden from the VOC. By 1700, Batavia had come to rely on the strength of Johor as a safeguard to the peaceful traffic of the Straits, a matter of vital interest to the Company because of the annual Company fleets which passed that way. The small fleet maintained at Malacca was insufficient to police the busy waterway, let alone attack Riau.[48] So Batavia had been content to turn a blind eye to those activities of Johor which harmed only Malacca. This had been a policy based on strength; Batavia's strength. But from 1714 it had become evident that the VOC was unable to enforce its will in the Straits. Its "alliance" with Johor had become an open mockery. This state of affairs held true for the remaining life of the VOC. Their stronghold at Malacca was to be kept at all costs (though complaints about these costs never ceased); but its direct influence on the surrounding area was to be negligible. The VOC held the town as much to prevent it from falling into any other European hands, as to provide any positive benefit for itself. The Malacca Straits would not, could not, be dealt with in the same fashion as areas within the Archipelago like Macassar or the Moluccas. In the eighteenth century the VOC, with its interest centered more and more on Java, found it impossible to dominate the area which had housed the great Malay polities of Malacca and Srivijaya. Even the attempt to use the good offices of Johor to maintain peace for the Company's activities in the area had broken down. The VOC retreated to a policy of strict neutrality, apparently content to become mere spectators in the unfolding drama of Malay politics.

NOTES

1. See Dampier, *Voyages and Discoveries,* 11, 118; Thomas Bowrey, *A Geographical Account of the Countries Round the Bay of Bengal, 1669 to 1679,* 259.

2. Raychaudhuri, *Jan Company in Coromandel,* 66.

3. D. N. Lewis, "The Last Malay Raja Muda of Johor," *JSEAS* 13.2 (1982): 222.

4. L. Andaya, *Kingdom of Johor,* 184.

5. *Daulat:* "majesty; the mysterious power which does not die with a Sultan, but returns to punish a degenerate successor." R. J. Wilkinson, *An Abridged Malay-English Dictionary,* 53. See L. Andaya, *Kingdom of Johor,* 189–190, for a cogent discussion of the importance of the death of Mahmud to the on-going politics of the Malay world.

6. Charles Lockyer, *An Account of the Trade in India,* 66.

7. Kol. Arch. 1603, Malacca to Batavia (25 January 1706)): 60. See Andaya, *Kingdom of Johor,* 205, for a detailed discussion of the failure of this mission and its unhelpful reception by Johor.

8. L. Andaya, *Kingdom of Johor,* 207, 210.

9. D. N. Lewis, "The Last Malay Raja Muda of Johor," 223.

10. L. Andaya, *Kingdom of Johor,* 104ff.

11. Kol. Arch. 1668, Governor Rooselaar's Memorie, (26 December 1709): 29.

12. See Appendix III.

13. Kol. Arch. 1673, Generale Missiven (29 November 1710): 132.

14. Kol. Arch. 1687, Malacca to Batavia (19 May 1710): 261.

15. Dampier, *Voyages,* 66.

16. Coolhaas, *Generale Missiven,* (3 November 1695): 740.

17. Batavia to Malacca (25 October 1710): 1354.

18. Kol. Arch. 1691, Generale Missiven (30 November 1711): 144.

19. Kol. Arch. 1706, Generale Missiven (15 November 1712): 137.

20. Kol. Arch. 1702, Malacca to Batavia, Raja Muda Mahmud and Sultan Abd al-Jalil to Governor Moerman (19 November 1711): 42-43.

21. Kol. Arch. 1708, Generale Missiven (13 January 1713): 1298.

22. Kol. Arch. 1719, Malacca to Batavia (3 January 1713): 40; Instructions to the Mission to Johor, 29-32.

23. This Raja Muda was also notable for his ventures in overseas trade. The details of some of these have survived. In 1701 he had sent a cargo to Bengal, and in 1708 another to Negapatnam. The latter involved a capital of about Sp. $8000. Another ship was sent to Macassar to buy spices to resell at Riau, and possibly one to China. In 1712 he was involved with the English country trader Alexander Hamilton in an attempt to sell a cargo of opium clandestinely at Malacca. Possibly because of the hostility he had generated in the VOC, his trading ventures do not seem to have been successful, though there may well have been others of which we are unaware. Certainly he was believed to be extremely wealthy in 1718. His adventure with Hamilton earned him the dislike of that less than impartial gentleman, who in return for his losses wrote most unflatteringly of Mahmud in his account of his voyages, helping to blacken the Johor ruler's reputation for nearly three centuries. See Alexander Hamilton, *A New Account of the East Indies* vol. 2: 53; and Lewis, "The Last Malay Raja Muda," 226–27, 231.

24. Kol. Arch. 1733, Malacca to Batavia (3 February 1713): 86-87.

25. Ibid. See also L. Andaya, *Kingdom of Johor,* 223.

26. Kol. Arch. 1706, Generale Missiven (15 November 1712): 136.

27. Kol. Arch. 1722, Generale Missiven (26 November 1713): 179.

28. Ibid.

29. The arrival of this mission was announced to Malacca in Batavia to Malacca (19 October 1713): 1082. E. Netscher reproduces the letter from the Mahmud to the Governor-General in *Djohor en Siak 1602–1865,* 44–45. The letter contains a request for an amount of gunpowder, a fairly normal matter between a Johor ruler and the VOC, which may have misled Netscher regarding the motives of this mission, which he interpreted as the last resort of a Johor desperately seeking allies.

30. Netscher, *Djohor,* xx-xxiii. This treaty is actually more important historiographically than historically. Netscher used its existence to argue that Johor was in total disarray and desperately in need of allies at this date, and willing to make major concessions to the VOC. In fact it was the VOC, not the Johorese, who were becoming weaker.

31. Indeed, Netscher concluded that they were.

32. Kol. Arch. 1724, Generale Missiven (11 January 1714): 2229.

33. Kol. Arch. 1737, Generale Missiven (26 November 1713): 173.

34. Kol. Arch. 1746, Malacca to Batavia (5 September 1714): 172.

35. Mahmud wrote to Malacca early in 1714 that he had been "too much

occupied with the Inderagiri war" to attend to the ratification, and protesting that he, the "sole ruler of Johoor, Pahang, and their respective subject territories," had been nowhere specifically mentioned in the treaty. Kol. Arch. 1746, Malacca to Batavia (12 March 1714): 114.

36. If the Johor ruler had really been eager for Dutch support, would not his chosen envoys have made sure that the treaty they carried away from Batavia was acceptable? Certainly Batavia had no motive to prolong the affair, and Company officials were by this time well aware of the delicacy of such matters in negotiations with Malay princes.

37. Kol. Arch. 1737, Generale Missiven (26 November 1714): 173.

38. This was learned afterwards from observers sent in 1715 to Riau. They reported that the spices were obtained in Ujung Padang, in Macassar, from Dutch and Chinese merchants of Ambon and Banda, and brought to Riau in ships bearing VOC passes. One ship at least had been fitted out by the Raja Muda. Kol. Arch. 1760, Report of Anthony van Aldorp on his visit to Riau. Malacca to Batavia (20 January 1716): 67ff. See also T. D. Hughes, "A Portuguese Account of Johore," *JMBRAS* 13.2 (1935): 125, 135. The amounts involved by 1715 were not such that Batavia felt driven to take immediate action, though it was plainly disturbed by this new aspect of Riau's trade.

39. Kol. Arch. 1746, Malacca to Batavia (12 August 1714): 134.

40. L. Andaya, *Kingdom of Johor,* 227–28.

41. Batavia to Malacca (26 June 1714): 533–36.

42. Kol. Arch. 1746, Malacca to Batavia (12 August 1714): 146–49. (See Translation in L Andaya, *Kingdom of Johor,* 332–33).

43. This fear was to be reiterated throughout the century, and to become a major factor in Batavia's decisions about Malacca.

44. Hall, *History of South East Asia,* 307.

45. Batavia to Malacca (7 June 1715): 623-26. Secret Letter to Governor Moerman.

46. Kol. Arch. 1764 Generale Missiven (30 November 1716): 210.

47. Ibid., and Kol. Arch. 1760, Malacca to Batavia (20 January 1716): 27ff.

48. Kol. Arch 1746, Malacca to Batavia (12 August 1714): 146–49.

3

THE DUTCH COMPANY AND THE BUGIS—OPTING FOR NEUTRALITY

As IF TO demonstrate the VOC's weakness, events in the Straits now took a different turn. For some time, groups of immigrant Bugis had been arriving in the Straits, driven from their homeland in southwest Sulawesi by persecution and turmoil, and eager to establish a new base. The Bugis had been emigrating since the overthrow of the Macassarese kingdom of Gowa in 1667 by the Dutch and their ally, Arung Palakka, the ruler of Bone.[1] A possible factor in this migration was "the new oppressive overlord-subject relationship introduced by . . . Arung Palakka, and enforced by the Dutch."[2] Several groups of Bugis were settled in the vicinity of Malacca by 1715, some even on VOC territory. They acted as mercenary soldiers, mined and traded and in general took advantage of the opportunities offered in the rich but relatively under-populated Malay Peninsula.[3] A number had settled in the tin-producing areas on the Linggi and Selangor Rivers, immediately north of Malacca. The newcomers had generally blended peacefully into the Malay scene, anxious to be left alone after their recent experiences in Sulawesi. In 1715, however, a quarrel arose between a group of Linggi-based Bugis and the Raja Muda of Johor, the overlord of that territory. These Bugis mercenaries, followers of one Daeng Marewah, had taken part in the recent Kedah civil war. The dispute which now arose concerned the division of their spoils, of which Mahmud claimed one-half as their territorial overlord.[4] The problem may have arisen out of a difference in Malay and Bugis custom on this head, for the Bugis were willing to concede the Raja Muda Mahmud a tenth of their loot, but not the full half he claimed. To the Bugis this demand unquestionably smacked of the very extortion they had left their homeland to escape. But to the Raja Muda it was surely an application of the power he had asserted since 1708, as the overlord of the Straits, to control the activities of all groups within his territories. Be that as it may, the Bugis would not submit to his demands, and this apparently minor dispute rapidly escalated into a full-blown confrontation.

It would seem that the lord of a powerful state like Johor would have little trouble in subduing a small group of immigrants, but from the first Mahmud met with no success in his attempts to bring the Bugis to heel. The force sent to drive them from Linggi was ignominiously defeated, and further defeats followed. Johor's tactics in controlling outlying *negari* were normally based on sea-power and the ability to cut off the trade. But this method was not sufficient in dealing with the Bugis, because from their base at Linggi they were able to reach the port of Malacca by overland routes. A successful attack by land, or the cooperation of the Dutch at Malacca, was necessary to defeat them. The Bugis were at this time perhaps the most accomplished land fighters in the Archipelago; they had been driven from their original homeland and were not prepared to leave their new country without a struggle.[5] Johor's efforts to dislodge them from Linggi and Selangor, the two tin producing areas north of Malacca in which they had settled, were embarrassingly unsuccessful. Repeated attacks met with repeated defeats, and the Raja Muda suffered a dangerous loss of prestige because of the continuing debacle.

The VOC watched their neighbors' quarrel closely, especially after September, 1715, when the Raja Muda finally ratified the new treaty between Johor and the VOC, and on the strength of this concession appealed to "his old friend and ally," the VOC, for help against the Bugis. This behavior may seem somewhat quixotic in view of his treatment of the VOC till then, and has been interpreted as a proof that by then Johor was already extremely weak and seeking a defensive alliance with the Dutch.[6] But this was demonstrably not the case, despite the problems caused by the Bugis; both the Dutch and independent

European observers at the Johor court as late as 1718 testify to the strength and wealth of the Johor ruler, and there is no indication that he saw himself as closely embattled.[7] This appeal was rather an attempt by the Raja Muda Mahmud to gain a very specific point from the VOC; he wanted the Dutch to close the port of Malacca to the Bugis.

The dominant or would-be dominant powers of the Malacca Straits had always been dependent on their control of trade. Only through the profits to be made from trade, both local and international, were these powers able to monopolize the wealth needed to hold in submission the minor communities of the area. A community such as the Bugis at Linggi should not have been able to withstand for long the overlord who controlled all the sea-borne trade in an area where most of the food had to be imported. The damaging military defeats suffered by the Johorese forces are explicable only if one realizes that the Raja Muda's forces were not designed to drive out an opponent bodily; it should have been sufficient to blockade the river mouth at Linggi to bring the Bugis to their knees, whatever their fighting skills and desperation. But the Bugis had direct overland access to the port of Malacca, and through this, to the supplies and munitions of the Archipelago; moreover, they controlled considerable supplies of tin, a product in great demand at Malacca, where the Dutch government sometimes found it very difficult to obtain even enough of the mineral to supply the immediate requirements of Batavia. To Malaccan officials already thoroughly disenchanted with Johor, the chance to exchange supplies of food (and even munitions) for Bugis tin was not to be lost. Short of attacking Malacca itself, which even Mahmud had shown no signs of contemplating, Johor's only recourse was direct military confrontation with the rebels, and an appeal to any remaining good will the VOC had for Johor to close their port to the Bugis.

But Dutch goodwill for Johor had been strained to its limit over the last five years; the Company wanted no part of this quarrel, and it declined to help the Raja Muda in any way. That is not to say that they saw this as an opportunity to finally punish Johor, though as recently as 1714 both Malacca and Batavia had been looking for ways to do this; even if such a course still appealed to Malacca, it obviously did not to Batavia, and both would have considered the Bugis far too dangerous an element to be used in this way. Though the Dutch had often used

Bugis as mercenary soldiers themselves, they did not welcome them as independent neighbors. This is quickly apparent from the tone taken by Governor Moerman in referring to the Bugis; pejorative terms such as "riff-raff," "scum," "pirates," and "sea-robbers" are commonly used in references to this group.[8] This is much harsher language than that generally applied to the Johorese. Whatever the Raja Muda had to fear from the Bugis it was not a combined Dutch/Bugis attack, for neither the Dutch of Malacca or Batavia ever felt inclined to ally themselves with the peninsular Bugis. On this they were for once in firm accord, and Governor Moerman's treatment of the Bugis clearly reflects this unswerving hostility. But they were equally unwilling to turn away the tin the Bugis brought in increasing quantities, quantities which succeeding Malaccan governments had striven in vain to collect for years past.

In March, 1716 a deputation from Daeng Marewah came to Malacca with the news that the Johorese were about to send another fleet against Linggi. Fearing the consequences of a renewed struggle, Daeng Marewah requested permission to move his people to join another Bugis settlement at Tangga Batu, an area within the jurisdiction of Malacca and thus under its protection, or to some other place under VOC protection.[9] These requests were "flatly refused," and Bugis subjects of the VOC were ordered not to help their kinsmen at Linggi. When Daeng Marewah subsequently came to Malacca in person, he was not even given an audience with the Governor. However, the Linggi Bugis were allowed to come to Malacca to buy provisions and sell tin, though the sale of gunpowder and munitions to them was officially strictly prohibited, in accordance with orders from Batavia.

The accord between Malacca and Batavia was still more apparent than real. The Malaccan government differed with Batavia over the question of dealing with the Bugis commercially. Batavia's first priority was to see the Bugis removed from this strategically delicate area, and the Governor-General and his Council stated candidly that they wished to see the Bugis driven out not only from Linggi, but from the whole vicinity of Malacca.[11] They did not believe that the quarrel between the Bugis and Johor could be of any conceivable benefit to the Company, and cautioned Malacca repeatedly to maintain the policy of strict neutrality, and give no cause of offense to either party. Their main fear appears once again to have been that the quarrel would drag the VOC into another fruitless war; or that the defeat of one of the protagonists would leave the victor too uncomfortably strong for the safety of the VOC's interests in the Straits. On the whole they favored the Raja Muda, who, they believed, held the advantage, and were concerned mostly with not offending him. They imposed a strict official embargo on the sale of gunpowder and munitions to the Bugis, and in 1718 they reprimanded Malacca for supplying Daeng Marewah with rice; but they did not forbid the purchase of tin from the Bugis.

Looking at the situation from the local rather than the overall view, Malacca had small reason to want to please the Raja Muda, and some individuals at Malacca obviously thought that, official policy or not, restricting this new trade with Linggi was taking neutrality too far. Distance between the two ports undoubtedly played its part here, as did the perpetual desire of the Company's servants to enhance their own fortunes even at the expense of their employer; and Daeng Marewah later stated that Malacca had been his chief source of provisions and munitions throughout the struggle.[12] Malacca had a powerful incentive to trade with the Bugis, for Daeng Marewah promised that the VOC would have all the tin production of Linggi and Selangor[13]—not a great sacrifice on the part of the Bugis, since the Raja Muda's fleets were blockading these places and cutting them off from alternative buyers, but a chance for profit that the Malaccan government, and even Batavia, found impossible to refuse.[14] For more than a decade tin collection at Malacca had not significantly bettered the 53,210 lbs obtained in 1716. But now the amounts soared; in 1717 the tally rose to 149,086 lbs, and for the next five years Malacca was able to send Batavia between 300,000 and 400,000 lbs annually.[15] It was the first time in the eighteenth century that Malacca had obtained enough of the mineral to satisfy even the demands of the European trade. Given this bargaining card, the Bugis were unlikely to be denied access to Malacca. So through 1716–17, though Dutch Malacca continued to refuse Daeng Marewah the formal aid or protection he kept seeking, the Bugis continued to bring tin openly to Malacca,[16] and to more or less clandestinely take home supplies.

The Raja Muda, having gone his own way against frequent protests from Malacca over the Siak and tin trades in previous years, was understandably unable to persuade Dutch Malacca to buy no tin from the

Bugis. And he was not able to take a high hand to prevent this trade, as he had done with Dutch trade in Siak, without open hostility against Malacca itself, for, unlike Siak, Linggi lay directly north of Malacca on the same coast. So in spite of the belief that they maintained the "strictest neutrality" in the Linggi/Johor dispute, and the obvious Dutch hostility to the Bugis, Dutch Malacca played a pivotal role in the survival of the Bugis settlement. Linggi and Selangor, like many settlements in the Peninsula, were based on tin-mining rather than agriculture, and were not self-sufficient. If the Raja Muda could have cut off their sale of tin and purchase of supplies, he could have brought the Bugis to their knees in spite of all their desperate bravery. The real struggle between the Bugis and the Raja Muda lay not so much in the pitched battles, but in the ability of the Bugis to keep their supply lines open, and this they were able to do because the European port of Malacca lay outside Johor's control.

The Raja Muda's struggle with the Bugis dragged on ignominiously through 1716–17. Continuing reverses undermined his prestige and considerably weakened his power over the *orang kaya* of the Johor court.[17] His concentration of trade in his own hands and his hard driving expansionist policies, impelled by the need to establish incontrovertibly the right of the Bendahara family to rule Johor, had made him enemies in the court as well as in Malacca. The shadow of the *derhaka*[18] of 1699 hung always over his head. The collapse of a proposed alliance with the Palembang prince Pangeran Dipati Anum led to new difficulties. Wild rumors of a possible attack from Aceh, then Siam, circulated.[19] In this situation Johor's leader was forced to soften his aggressive policies in other areas and become more conciliatory to his opponents within the court. Under pressure from the *orang kaya,* the royal residence was removed in 1716 from Riau to the Johor mainland, an uncharacteristically defensive gesture for Mahmud.

In the wake of this retreat, possibly encouraged by it, a new rebellion arose among the disaffected Minangkabaus of Siak, whose trade with Malacca Mahmud had been restricting for the last ten years. This rebellion came to a head in 1718, under the astute leadership of Raja Kecik, who claimed to be the posthumous son of the last ruler of the old Malacca line, Sultan Mahmud, murdered in 1699. His claim, though rejected by contemporary Dutch officials and later historians of the period, was one which would have appealed to those contemporary elements of Johor society still deeply disturbed by the murder of the sultan, and thus was calculated to cause the maximum disruption among the disaffected elements of Johor's court.

There is no indication that the Dutch believed that the Raja Muda faced any substantial threat between 1716 and 1718, and Malacca appears to have been caught totally off guard when the news came from Johor in March, 1718 that the Minangkabaus had stormed and captured the town.[20] The invaders were aided by the treachery of some members of the Johor *orang kaya,* and by the carefully fostered rumor of Raja Kecik's alleged descent from the old Malacca line. Raja Muda Mahmud, betrayed by a large part of his forces, died fighting. His brother Sultan Abd al-Jalil abdicated (he later escaped temporarily to Pahang, where he was slain by Kecik's forces in 1721), and the Bendahara fled, seeking refuge at Malacca in April, 1718.[21]

The fall of the Raja Muda in 1718 radically changed the situation the Dutch faced in the Straits of Malacca. In place of a strong, if at times overbearing, Johor, they now had to deal with three groups vying for power; the Bugis, that portion of the Johorese who still supported Abd al-Jalil, and the supporters of Raja Kecik, both Johorese and Minangkabau. Conditions were chaotic. The Dutch, taken by surprise, clung to their neutrality, though in Malacca feelings towards the Bugis steadily deteriorated, as the latter's actions reflected their rapidly lessening need of the Dutch port.

Malacca's attitude to the Bugis, which had been relatively cordial as long as they were willing tin suppliers, now rapidly caught Batavia's tone of open hostility. The reversal of the goodwill previously shown to Malacca by the Bugis was abrupt; as early as September, 1718 Moerman wrote to Daeng Marewah about the "faithless and piratical behavior" of his Bugis, who were now ruining the trade of Malacca's freeburghers. The foreshores of Malacca had been made unsafe by cruising Bugis vessels; Javanese merchants carrying rice to the Dutch port had been "lured away." Moerman demanded that the Bugis "return to their homeland."[22] With the fall of the Raja Muda the Bugis position was much stronger; and their numbers had been augmented in late 1718 by an alliance with the previous Bendahara of Johor and a large section of his followers, who were desperately seeking ways to free Johor of the Siak invaders. Their combined forces had raided in the vicinity of Bengkalis.[23]

Batavia, on the other hand, though no less hostile to the newcomers than before, was also re-evaluating its attitudes in view of the changing situation. The same need to appease a potentially powerful opponent that had colored their relations with the Raja Muda now began to appear in their treatment of the Bugis. They warned Malacca that the need to be wary in dealings with the Bugis and not to give offense had increased, not lessened. They "wished the Governor-in-Council had used more prudent language in their letter to Daeng Marewah."[24] Batavia, as much as in 1714 and 1716, wanted at all costs to prevent an open rupture with any local power. There was to be no attempt by the Dutch to manipulate these events in the Straits of Malacca for their own benefit; they seem to have thought merely in terms of survival. Batavia assured Malacca that the Bugis would not constitute an active threat to Malacca itself, as long as the government was careful not to become involved in local quarrels.

The Malacca government was left in something of a quandary by this policy—a situation that was to become more apparent as the century progressed. On the one hand, they were pressed to take no part in local affairs; on the other, Batavia still required that they support their own costs as far as possible by trade. Given the intertwining of trade and politics in this region, the pitfalls are apparent. For the time being, however, the disruption among the Malay forces was such that Malacca continued to prosper modestly. Politically, the policy of neutrality was strictly pursued. Malacca continued to refuse all overtures for alliance, but remained open commercially to Malay and Bugis alike.

The defeated Sultan of Johor, Abd al-Jalil, appealed to Malacca for aid against his enemies in the name of the old treaty of friendship and alliance between the VOC and Johor.[25] The deposed ruler had fled from Pahang north to Trengganu, and was seeking help from the Dutch, English, and French, or anyone who could give it. Malacca replied that Johor had shown little inclination to abide by this treaty in the course of the last two decades, and therefore they did not feel bound to help the Johor ruler in his need. His appeared the weakest of the three power groups. Malacca commented in 1721 that even his adherents did not seem to expend much effort on his behalf, and it certainly was not tempted to support Abd al-Jalil's cause.

Of the three groups, Malacca might be expected to have been most sympathetic to the Minangkabaus from Siak, because of Malacca's strong commercial links with the area. But the Malacca government resisted the appeals of Raja Kecik for support, both before and after his attack on Johor. In 1717 he had asked to be supplied with gunpowder, threatening to disrupt the trade of Siak if his demands were not met. He sent Malacca a letter, which purported to come from the ruler of the Minangkabaus in Pagar Ruyung, but was considered by the administration to be fraudulent and ignored.[26] The request for aid was officially denied, but no reprisals from Siak followed. Malacca was not impressed by Raja Kecik's claim to be a scion of the old Malacca dynasty, or by his other claims of support from the rulers of Pagar Ruyung.[27] Further attempts by Raja Kecik to gain an alliance with Malacca against the Bugis, who after 1719 had become allied with some elements of the old court of Johor and were attempting to drive Raja Kecik out of Johor, were repeatedly refused. In 1719 the then Governor-General wrote that no alliance with Raja Kecik could be contemplated, and that if he raised the matter again he must be referred to Batavia.[28]

Malacca was now feeling the loss of the policing abilities of a strong Johorese regime, as the Straits continued to be a battlefield for the opposing factions. In 1721 there were reports of "outrageous piracy of the Bugis, which is carried on without fear by land and sea quite near this fortress."[29] Several Malaccan soldiers, and even a private citizen of the town, had been seized by Bugis marauders on the outskirts to be sold as slaves. The Malaccan Malay community had become so fearful of the Bugis that they would not venture out to sea to fish, or go to tend their gardens outside the city. Malacca was beginning to suffer from a shortage of fresh foods.

To remedy this Batavia sent out the Company sloop *Goram* to police the foreshores of Malacca and "to board all vessels not furnished with [VOC] passes and search them." The sloop met three of Daeng Marewah's vessels without passes; the Bugis crews would not submit to a search; they were overpowered, and their ships were sunk. Daeng Marewah wrote to Malacca in protest, but Governor van Suchtelen rejected his complaint. The Governor believed that only violence and brutality were to be expected from the Bugis; he feared that they would so intimidate the local population that no one would dare stand up to them.[30] This view of the Bugis was not softened by the discovery that they were in correspondence with the ruler of Bone, to whom they had declared their allegiance, and from whom they sought reinforcements.[31] In view of this, the *Goram* was once more sent out to patrol the coast for forty miles around Malacca, supported by a vessel owned by a Malaccan freeburgher. But these were all defensive moves, aimed to protect Malacca, not to extend the VOC's influence in the Straits; Batavia had made it quite clear that this conflict was to be played out without Dutch intervention.

In 1721, news came to Malacca that the exiled Sultan Abd al-Jalil had been murdered in Pahang by Raja Kecik's men. This was followed by the (for Malacca) even more alarming tidings, received in early 1722, that Daeng Marewah's forces had driven Raja Kecik out of Riau, and installed Abd al-Jalil's son, Sulaiman, on the throne of Johor. "A new king called Sulaiman" had been "created" by the Bugis, and, in return for their support, they had been allowed to take up the mantle last worn by Sulaiman's uncle Mahmud, along with the great powers he had accumulated. Sulaiman had installed Daeng Marewah as "Yang dipertuan Muda [Raja Muda], to govern the kingdom of Johor and Pahang and Riau and all the subject territories with absolute authority."[32]

This situation greatly disadvantaged Malacca; "for now the Bugis scum will be supported in their piracies."[33] As van Suchtelen realized, this alliance gave the Bugis the immense benefit of being able to call on a legitimate, traditional Malay source of authority. He feared the worst from this combination and advised his superiors that Daeng Marewah would now surely become more bold and arrogant in his success, "which can bring nothing but misfortune to the Malaccan merchants; for it does not appear that the piracies of this Bugis scum shall cease."[34] He also pressed for a more active policy to restrain this growing threat to the VOC's interests in the Straits. Malacca had previously "held within the limits of strict neutrality, without showing the least partiality [to any of the warring factions] but on the contrary seeking to be fair to both sides."[35] But now van Suchtelen believed that the Bugis had become a threat to Malacca itself. There were rumors of a projected Bugis attack on the Dutch fortress. As in 1714, Malacca was helpless against a strong local adversary. Hoping to rid the Straits of the Bugis scourge in the guise of protecting the establishment at Malacca, van Suchtelen sent reports to Batavia of the forces available to the Bugis, and the estimated reinforcements required to drive them from the area.

But Batavia had no enthusiasm for his plan. Such an operation would have cost the Company dearly,[36] and with continuing conflicts in Java and now in Palembang, its resources were ever more thinly stretched. The decline of the VOC was still not apparent to the world at large, but the time was past when Batavia was willing to risk its fortunes on such adventures. Experience in the Straits of Malacca had shown that little profit was to be had in the area, however much was spent. The policy of neutrality offered the best hope of protecting the valuable strategic post of Malacca without entering into rash expenditure, and van Suchtelen was ordered once more to pursue it diligently. He was severely rebuked for even asking advice about "choosing a king for the Johorese lands, where the Company had no property or settlement."[37] The VOC would not meddle in Malay politics. But nor would it risk the loss of Malacca; in recognition of the dangers posed to its outpost by the growing unrest in the Straits, Batavia sent a further 100 European soldiers to reinforce Malacca's garrison of 439.[38]

The continuing neutrality of the VOC in 1722 was of great importance to Daeng Marewah's Bugis. It probably guaranteed their ascendancy in the Straits, for, with the Johorese establishment still disrupted by the rivalries springing from the violent ending of the old Malacca dynasty in 1699 and the Raja Muda Mahmud's subsequent aggressive policies, no other group was strong enough to oppose the single-minded immigrants. Their capture of Riau and alliance with Sulaiman gave them the machinery to exploit all the profitable aspects of the Malay port-kingdom system, a system which their own wide commercial contacts in the Archipelago could only enhance. Malacca's determined neutrality was certainly a disappointment to Raja Kecik, who, given the open hostility of the Dutch to the Bugis, must have hoped for some relief from this quarter. Any schemes which had been harbored by Sultan Sulaiman and his Malay supporters to use the Dutch to drive out the Bugis once Riau was regained (Sulaiman approached Malacca on precisely this matter in 1723) were also doomed to disappointment.[39] Though the conflict with Raja Kecik continued, during the 1720s the Bugis, helped by strategic marriages with the Malay *orang kaya,* were able to weave themselves into the political structure of Johor without hindrance from the Dutch at Malacca.[40] Their moment of weakness was ignored, for the hopes and ambitions of the Company were now firmly settled in Java, and expensive adventures in the Straits of Malacca were not even to be contemplated.

And initially Malacca fared well from the collapse of the old Johor polity, despite Governor van Suchtelen's misgivings. The town was not attacked, for as neither the Bugis nor Raja Kecik was able to obtain an absolute victory, neither faction could afford to bring a new enemy down upon itself. Despite the dangers caused by the constant skirmishing of the warring parties, Malacca's earnings did not substantially decline in these years.[41] Tin continued to be brought to Malacca, probably the only safe port in the area, in considerable amounts until 1726, and even after this date an occasional windfall cargo would arrive from Selangor or Linggi, as groups of Bugis in these areas fell out with their overlords in Riau. Trade with Siak was flourishing; Raja Kecik, faced with the rejuvenated Bugis-backed Johor, could not afford to antagonize the VOC, and placed no hindrance in the way of Malacca's merchants.[42] The Manila trade (the sale of spices at Malacca to merchants from India bound to Manila,) which had been gravely threatened by the Raja Muda's experiments in the spice trade at Riau, was once more bringing in a healthy revenue. The number of both foreign and local vessels entering Malacca increased after 1718, for the Dutch port was a relatively stable island in the war-torn sea of the Straits in the 1720s. The surrounding ports remained unsafe; the lack of a strong Johorese fleet to patrol the seas and ensure the safety of the passing trading vessels was compounded by the need of the rival factions to attract as much trade as possible to their own ports, by whatever means. In this situation Malacca, protected by the VOC, had some advantages, and the port fared better than it had in the days of Johor's prosperity.

Batavia was perfectly content with this state of affairs, so long as the port of Malacca itself was not endangered. Steps were taken to prevent this from happening—it has been noted that in 1722 substantial reinforcements were sent to the garrison, and also an unusually large amount was spent on repairs to the fortress.[43] Whenever possible, armed vessels were sent to protect Malacca's trade from the marauding Bugis and Siak fleets. The decision was made in 1721 to send an annual expedition to the Dindings [Pulau Pangkor], off the coast of Perak, where a Dutch outpost had existed from 1670 to 1690,[44] to protect the VOC's rights to the abandoned fort, and to keep it out of the hands of the Bugis or Minangkabaus, or any European power. On several occasions the patrol broke up settlements near the old fort, and in 1724 the *Patena* met a hostile group of Bugis at the site.[45] But these actions were merely defensive, and any temptation on Malacca's part to influence the ongoing conflict was effectively countered by Batavian opposition. Neutrality was to be maintained at all costs.

Most of Malacca's problems related to the battle between the warring factions to control the local and passing trade, the main source of revenue for any potential power in the Straits. What the Dutch saw as the "piratical" attempts of the warring factions to re-direct trade were actually more important than the battles that were fought. An example of this is the story of a Chinese merchant in 1723 who was stopped by Daeng Marewah near the Kelang point en route to Malacca. The Bugis chief gave him a pass and told him that if he went straight to Selangor he would not be molested again. He ignored the threat and continued to Malacca, but others similarly placed may have acted differently.[46] This was the crucial struggle of the war. The Bugis chronicle the *Tuhfat al Nafis* states that food became very expensive in Riau during Raja Kecik's attacks, "because the state was in confusion," and no rice was brought from Java or Bali.[47]

Gradually conditions in the Straits returned to a more peaceful footing as the Bugis consolidated their power. In early 1728 the Bugis won a decisive victory over Raja Kecik. On the death of the Raja Muda Daeng Marewah in October of the same year, his brother, Daeng Cellak, was installed in his place, and the Bugis seemed assured of retaining their position in Johor.[48] Riau's trade began to revive. But one rift in the Johor polity caused by the rebellion of 1718 did not heal, and the Bugis, though secure in Riau, did not regain control of the Siak area from Raja Kecik or his heirs. Here again, despite their persistent pursuit of a policy of neutrality, the Dutch played a part. After 1722 the Malaccan government did not renew its call to move against the Bugis, though feelings towards them did not soften, and Malacca steadfastly refused the overtures of Raja Kecik to ally with him against the common enemy. But Siak was vital to the well-being of Malacca, as events of 1709–1714 had shown, and Malacca did on several occasions, with the approval of Batavia, supply the Siak forces with gunpowder and other munitions;[49] it was in their interests to keep Siak independent of Riau.

The strong trade between Malacca and Siak allowed the latter to remain independent of the Riau Bugis. From the collapse of the old Johor Empire Malacca had gained free and unhindered access to Siak, whose trade had been so important to the Dutch port's financial viability, and so vulnerable to a strong Johor.

The situation remained static for almost two decades after 1722. One of the most notable aspects of Malacca's correspondence in the late 1720s and the 1730s is the lack of detail about local affairs, in contrast to the abundant information (often in the form of complaints) of earlier periods. Malacca was consigned to inactivity and insignificance, a minor port, its officials minding their own business as they had been told, busying themselves with making their own fortunes (not always in the ways approved by their masters). Malay and Bugis sources hint at important events in Johor, the growing unrest between Malay and Bugis factions there, but the Dutch are largely silent. Since 1714 Malacca's masters at Batavia had made it clear that the Company wanted nothing from the Straits of Malacca but to keep the ancient town and fortress out of any other hands. Again and again the theme was reiterated. Nothing must be undertaken which could conceivably lead the Company into a potentially costly war in this area of peripheral interest. Malaccan governments could only observe—and profit, where possible, from the unusual windfalls of trade which came their way when one or other of the local combatants found it convenient to bring their tin to market.

Europeans had never been further from dominating the Straits of Malacca. And yet, paradoxically, it may have been the Dutch in Malacca who had a decisive part in shaping the new lines of confrontation. For Dutch Malacca had allowed the Bugis to endure the assaults of powerful Johor, and may well have been a deciding factor in Siak's emergence as an independent separate state. The continued existence of their port at Malacca was all the Dutch required, but this in itself was an anomaly in the traditional pattern of Straits politics, where, ideally, the dominant polity drew all trade to its own port, or only allowed such ports as Selangor to continue as mere subjects. Dutch Malacca would be subject to no Malay ruler, and did not or would not see how important this control of the local trade was to Malay politics. The seemingly smooth emergence of the Johor Empire as the dominant Malay polity was disrupted by the existence of a European port outside its control. In the midst of their most ineffectual period in the history of their contact with the Straits, the Dutch presence in Malacca had had a telling influence on political developments in the Malay world.

NOTES

1. The tendency is to refer to Bugis as monolithic group. This was not the case—there were several factions among the Bugis. See Lewis, "The Dutch East India Company and the Straits of Malacca, 1700–1784," 159-60; and L. Andaya, *Kingdom of Johor,* 297. One group was led by the famous "five brothers" from Bone, whose story was recorded by their descendant Raja Ali Haji ibn Ahmad in his *Tuhfat al-Nafis.*

2. L. Andaya, *Kingdom of Johor,* 117; see also his *The Heritage of Arung Palakka.*

3. Some were employed by the Raja Muda himself, and still others participated in the budding spice trade between Riau and the eastern archipelago. Hughes, "A Portuguese Account of Johore," 110–56.

4. L. Andaya, *Kingdom of Johor,* 231. Kol. Arch. 1760, Report of Anthony van Aldorp on his visit to Riau (28 December 1715): 118–19.

5. L. Andaya, *Kingdom of Johor,* 235.

6. Ibid. 236; Netscher, Djohor, pp. 43–46.

7. Hughes, "A Portuguese Account," 120–121. Note the recurring story of Mahmud's preoccupation with a game of chess at the time of the Minangkabau invasion of Johor in 1718; the story hardly applies to a man expecting defeat. See Raja Ali Haji ibn Ahmad, *The Precious Gift,* 49.

8. See e.g. Kol. Arch. 1751, Generale Missiven (28 November 1715): 430, and Kol. Arch. 1775, Malacca to Batavia (16 March 1716): 6.

9. Kol. Arch. 1775, Malacca to Batavia (16 March 1716): 5.

10. Kol. Arch. 1787, Governor Moerman's Memorie (1717): 69.

11. Kol. Arch. 1751, Generale Missiven (28 November 1715): 430.

12. Kol. Arch. 1853; Malacca to Batavia, Daeng Marewah to the Governor of Malacca, (11 March 1721): 69.

13. Kol. Arch. 1775, Malacca to Batavia (20 August 1717): 56.

14. Kol. Arch. 1779, Generale Missiven (30 November 1717).

15. D. N. Lewis, "The Tin Trade" *New Zealand Journal of History* 3.1 (1969): 60. Obviously not all this tin came from the Bugis territories after 1718.

16. Kol. Arch. 1779, Generale Missiven (30 November 1717); and Kol. Arch. 1853, Malacca to Batavia (11 March 1923): 69.

17. Lewis, "The Last Malay Raja Muda,": 231.

18. Derhaka; treason, especially against a ruler. The murder of Mahmud in 1699 loosened the ties which bound the Johor political structure.

19. The Malacca government believed that these rumors had been spread by

Johor itself, to help persuade the VOC to cooperate in dislodging the Bugis. Kol. Arch. 1764, Generale Missiven (30 November 1716): 211.

20. Kol. Arch. 1803, Malacca to Batavia (4 July 1718): 25.

21. Ibid. Bendahara's Report to Malacca, (26 May 1718): 27–28.

22. Kol. Arch. 1803, Malacca to Batavia, Governor Moerman to Daeng Marewah (28 September 1718): 112.

23. Kol. Arch. 1803, Malacca to Batavia (28 September 1718): 20.

24. Batavia to Malacca (19 August 1719): 835.

25. Kol. Arch. 1803, Malacca to Batavia; Sultan Abd al-Jalil to Governor van Suchtelen (22 January 1719): 15.

26. Kol. Arch. 1787, Malacca to Batavia (30 January 1718): 42.

27. L. Andaya, "Raja Kecik and the Minangkabau Conquest of Kingdom in 1718," *JMBRAS*, 45.2 (1972): 51–75.

28. Batavia to Malacca, (19 August 1719): 838.

29. Kol. Arch. 1872, Malacca to Batavia (11 March 1722): 42.

30. Ibid. 42–46.

31. L. Andaya, *Kingdom of Johor,* 290.

32. Raja Ali Haji ibn Ahmad, *The Precious Gift,* 64.

33. Kol. Arch. 1872, Malacca to Batavia (24 March 1722): 73.

34. Ibid. 76.

35. Kol. Arch. 1853, Malacca to Batavia (27 August 1721): 80.

36. Kol. Arch. 1864, Generale Missiven (19 March 1722): 3.

37. van der Chijs, *Realia* 2: 180. Resolution 10 May 1723.

38. Batavia to Malacca (18 October 1722): 606.

39. The only indication in the VOC's records of an attempt by Sultan Sulaiman to oust his Bugis supporters comes in 1724, when the Governor-General wrote to the Gentlemen that "as it had been decided that any move against the Bugis would be unsuccessful, the Malaccan authorities had refused a request from Raja Kecik and Sultan Sulaiman that the VOC join forces with them against the Bugis." Kol. Arch 1893, Generale Missiven (30 November 1924): 848. See Kol. Arch. 1888, Malacca to Batavia (11 October 1923): 22, for references to copies of the letters from Sulaiman and Kecik.

40. L. Andaya, *Kingdom of Johor,* 279ff.

41. See Appendix II.

42. On the one occasion when he did try to embargo Malacca's trade in Siak, Raja Kekik "was given an unexpected jolt" by his subjects. L. Andaya, *Kingdom of Johor,* 286–87.

43. See Appendix II. 1722 expenditure was f172601, an increase of nearly 20 percent over the previous year's outlay. Kol. Arch. 1888, Malacca to Batavia (30 January 1724): 8.

44. Kol. Arch. 1853, Malacca to Batavia (27 August 1721): 78.

45. Kol. Arch. 1905, Malacca to Batavia (30 January 1725): 14.

46. Kol. Arch. 1888, Malacca to Batavia (29 March 1723): 5.

47. Raja Ali Haji ibn Ahmad, *The Precious Gift,* 70.

48. L. Andaya, *Kingdom of Johor,* 312.

49. Kol. Arch. 1911, Generale Missiven (30 November 1725) 642; Kol. Arch. 1966, van Suchtelen's Memorie (1727): 41.

4

THE DUTCH ALLIANCE
WITH THE MALAYS

By the end of the first quarter of the eighteenth century, the VOC
had settled on a commercial policy in the Straits that totally suppressed
Malacca. At no time during the life of the Company did this policy
alter.[1] The competition of the well established Asian and foreign
European traders for the tin, gold, and pepper of the Straits, and for the
profits to be made from the sale of cloth and opium there, was too strong
to make it worth the VOC's while to attempt to subdue this troublesome
area. Malacca was to remain strictly neutral in the affairs of the Straits.

The cataclysm of 1718 had finally laid to rest the old order in the
Straits, which had relied on a single dominant port and used the economic power of this port to set up a political empire. The failure of the
Bendahara family to establish a new Johor Empire was underlined in
the 1720s by the reliance of the new Sultan Sulaiman (son of the late
Sultan Abd al-Jalil) on the Bugis to recapture his court and regalia, in
the absence of support from more traditional Malay forces.[2] Siak
remained alienated, in control of another immigrant group, the
Minangkabaus. In time all these wounds may have healed, and, as
doubtless had happened many times in the past, these immigrants
would have come to consider themselves Malay, and reverted to the old
power structure based on the economic dynamics of the region. But
time was not available, as the world moved into a period when the old

patterns gave way to new, and European technology prepared to place its stamp over the globe. Because of this the Johor that the Bugis helped resurrect in the 1730s differed in certain important aspects from the Johor of the Malay Raja Muda Mahmud.

The Bugis were less interested, at least for the time being, in the domination of all Malay ports and hinterlands than in the structuring of an Archipelago-wide trade, using their farflung family contacts in Sulawesi [Celebes], Kalimantan [Borneo], and even Java, to collect at Riau the products which were now in growing demand among a new set of merchants to the Straits, the English country traders. Here we intersect another important change in the conditions of Asian trade which was to drag the VOC's attention willynilly back to the Straits of Malacca.

European patterns of consumption were changing, and the virtual monopoly of the sale of pepper and spices to Europe that it had enjoyed in the seventeenth century was no longer enough to guarantee the VOC a profit. Chinese products were becoming increasingly important to the European consumer. But once more European merchants came up against the exchange problem—they had little to offer the Chinese in return for the porcelain and tea that were so much in demand in the West. However, Indian and Southeast Asian goods, such as opium and tin, had always been in demand in China, and so Europeans, especially the English, began to trade between India, the Straits of Malacca, and China (cloth and opium from India to the Straits for tin, tin and opium for tea and porcelain).[3] As a result, the volume of European (and Asian) vessels passing through the Straits of Malacca each year was substantially increasing.[4]

The VOC, bound by a century of habit and a vast and expensive network of possessions and bureaucracy, was slow to enter this new field, and found itself more and more unable to compete with the English Company, which was backed by the growing commercial power of eighteenth-century England. The Dutch Company had been declining financially since the end of the previous century. After 1725 it ceased to show an overall profit, and thereafter went steadily deeper into debt.[5] The 1740s saw a questioning of VOC policy at its highest levels, as the Directors tried to stem this tide of losses. But the old dog could not learn new tricks; the Directors blamed this decline on the incompetence and corruption of the Company's servants in the East, rather than their own monopolistic policies.

In 1743, in the hope of putting an end to many of the problems facing them in the East, the Directors appointed the energetic Gustave Van Imhoff Governor-General. Van Imhoff claimed to have solutions to the Company's woes, and seemed prepared to pursue them in a vigorous manner. He had written a lengthy memorandum on the subject, presented to the Heeren Zeventien in 1741.[6] Many of his reforms concentrated on Java, but he did also attempt to address the illicit private trading and smuggling which the Directors believed to be the main cause of the Company's economic decline. He proposed to combat this by a new approach to the VOC's inter-Asian trade; he advocated the opening of sections of that trade to free citizens and Asian traders, arguing that the VOC must withdraw from the smaller sectors of Asian trade where it had never been able to compete successfully with the independent merchants. He persuaded the Directors to open the inland and sea trade between the Archipelago and India to the freeburghers and resident Asian traders of the VOC's establishments, arguing that the Company would profit from the the revenue of this increased trade. However, he did not confront the problem of the Company's stultifying monopolistic practices; trade between the VOC's ports was still to be restricted, and each voyage had to begin and end at Batavia, direct commerce between the other ports remaining forbidden. Van Imhoff also established the Opium Society, with sole rights of trading in opium within the VOC's territories. The emphasis of his administration was on reform and innovative policies in an attempt to stop the now obvious decline of the VOC.[7]

Van Imhoff's impact on Malacca came more in the context of his new climate of vigor and reform than in any specific change of policy. The Company's government at Malacca was unquestionably ripe for reform. The Directors had been complaining for a decade that Malacca was a *lastpost,* a drain on the Company's dwindling resources. During the 1730s, tin and gold deliveries declined significantly, along with other branches of Malacca's trade. The policy of strict neutrality in local affairs had degenerated on the part of the Company's servants into an excuse for complete inactivity and lack of commercial initiative (at least in the Company's affairs). In 1743 the retiring governor, Rogier de

Laver, was arrested on suspicion of corruption, and two commissioners were sent to look into the Company's affairs in Malacca. Their investigations lasted almost a year, and they made a lengthy report on the instances of corruption that had been uncovered. Tin smuggling had been practiced "grossly and greatly" by members of the Malaccan government.[8] De Laver and his colleagues had also traded illicitly in opium and pepper, and used Company vessels for private trade. They had defrauded the port of tolls and other taxes. In short, the officers of the Malaccan Government had themselves become one with the many competitors whom they continued to blame for ruining the Company's trade in the Straits.

Having thus uncovered and, he hoped, put an end to the grosser corruption in the Malacca government, Governor-General Van Imhoff turned his attention to the problem of making Malacca pay its way. In keeping with his ideas for the general revitalization of the Company's trade, he suggested that it might be possible to "extract a profit from [local] products or domestic trade to other places *which does not prejudice the Company's trade*" so as to "make the upkeep of such an important fortress more tolerable for the Company."[9] The free merchants of Malacca were to be allowed to participate in the trade provided that they sold their purchases only to the Company.[10] Positive steps were also taken to encourage the future honesty and diligence of the VOC's servants. A new rule allowing Malaccan officials a proportion of the profit of the customs duties, allotted according to rank, was instituted, to discourage fraud in this area.[11] Governors were to receive 2 rds per bahar for all tin delivered to the Company from outside Malacca's territories. An increase in the price of gold was authorized, and Governor Willem Bernard Albinus, the new head of the Malaccan establishment, was urged to take all possible positive steps to bring about a revival of trade.[12]

None of these measures went any distance towards solving the real problems of Malacca's inability to compete with the Asian and other European merchants in the Straits. For that, a far more radical approach to Company policy would have been necessary. Van Imhoff's suggestions for the improvement of the tin trade echoed the time-honored pattern, advising the Malaccan government to increase its share in the trade by reducing the amounts of tin being exported by other merchants; in 1745 Albinus was admonished "to take care that all the tin of

Nanning . . . and the Malaccan hinterlands falls to the Company."[13] The VOC had profited very little from the tin trade at Malacca in the 1730s. In 1744 the Batavian government passed a significantly worded resolution that "the tin trade should not be abandoned," but again no formula was provided to help the Malaccan government overcome the handicap—itself imposed by Batavia—of being unable to offer a realistic price for the tin.

All of this may have had no great effect on Malacca, but for the fact that the political situation in the Malay states was so patently ripe for interference. The neighboring Malay communities were recovering from the fragmentation of Johor, which had left the immigrant Bugis in a position of great power. As the quarrel with Raja Kecik subsided in the 1730s and the Straits became more peaceful, the new Johor reasserted itself as a powerful force in the Straits. Riau had again become a regular port of call for the ever-growing number of European independent merchants en route to China, as witness the Malaccan authorities' complaints about large amounts of tin and pepper diverted to these merchants via the Bugis ports.[14] But the great Malay families who had in the past controlled the revenues of this trade had been largely ousted from the Johor court by the immigrant Bugis. The Bugis forces had won back the Johor regalia and the port of Riau for the current sultan, Sulaiman, and in return, after his installation as Sultan of Johor in 1722, he had granted them the office of Raja Muda in perpetuity. Not only the rank, but the large powers—unusual in the Malay traditional political structure—that his uncle the Raja Muda Mahmud had enjoyed.[15] By the 1740s feelings in the Johor court ran high between Malays and Bugis. The Malays of Johor were looking for a means to rid themselves of their now unwanted allies, and other Malay princes of the Straits area had also begun to fear the growing power of the immigrants. Relations between the Bugis at Selangor and Riau and the Malays of the Johor court were becoming increasingly strained. There is evidence of only one occasion on which Sultan Sulaiman himself fell out with his Bugis allies, and that was quite early in their association.[16] But the Malay *orang kaya* at the court of Johor were openly hostile to the Bugis. In 1729 Sulaiman's daughter had married the son of the ruler of Trengganu, Raja Mansur Syah. This prince joined the court at Riau, where he became a leader of the Malay faction.[17]

The Bugis, having once more made Riau the site of the court and the central port of Johor, were, in the time-honored way of the Malacca Straits, actively encouraging its trade. In 1743 their "piratical activities" were "daily increasing." The previous year they had boldly attacked a French ship bound for Manila; and Daeng Cellak's attempt to re-route Chinese trade has been noted above.[18] Unlike earlier Malay powers, however, the Bugis did not confine their activities to one port. They were also developing the port of Selangor, in the territory north of Malacca, where they had established their main homeland in the Peninsula, and they had begun the practice of gambier cultivation on the island of Bintan.[19]

The Batavian government had never had a good opinion of the Bugis, but after the Raja Muda failed to drive them out of the Straits, Batavia had shown more concern for staying on peaceful terms with the Bugis than for opposing their rise to power in Johor. Throughout the 1720s and 1730s this remained a settled policy. By the 1740s, however, the increasingly widespread activity of the Bugis in the Archipelago was causing Batavia mounting concern. In July, 1744 Governor-General Van Imhoff wrote to Sultan Sulaiman of Johor, complaining of the "piratical habits" of some of his subjects. They were, he complained, making the sea unsafe in many places, trading without passes or permission from the VOC to Kalimantan, Sulawesi, and other islands to which the Company had prohibited trade, and carrying out all sorts of smuggling activities. These same individuals also allegedly "forgot themselves" so far as to come yearly to the coast of Java "even within sight of this town [Batavia]" to raid, steal, and otherwise molest passing vessels. Van Imhoff observed that though he and his council wished to believe that these misdeeds were committed without the knowledge of Sultan Sulaiman, whose friendship they had no desire to lose, nevertheless, he must insist that the Johor ruler put an end to this state of affairs. In addition, Van Imhoff took the opportunity to inform Sulaiman of a new restriction they had imposed on trade to Java. All shipping bound for ports in Java must first call at Batavia or risk confiscation of their cargo and vessel. This restriction was a result of an attempt to stamp out the smuggling of opium and cloth from the Straits area, where it was brought by the Asian and European traders from India into Java.[20]

Johor's reply was not conciliatory. Letters were sent to Batavia in the name of both Sultan Sulaiman and the Bugis Raja Muda Daeng Cellak, but the two letters are essentially identical, and almost certainly express Daeng Cellak's views. They deny all knowledge of "piratical" activities and claim that the understanding between Johor and the VOC had been "exactly maintained"; finally, there is a counter-complaint concerning the treatment of certain Johor subjects at Semarang.[21] The Bugis were even less conciliatory than the Malay Johor leaders had been in their dealings with Batavia in the past, perhaps because of a perception that the Company was weakening throughout the Archipelago, perhaps because the Company had stayed so determinedly neutral in Straits affairs since 1720. Their reply was not calculated to appease the proud and active Van Imhoff.

By 1745 the situation had grown so critical that the Batavian authorities felt compelled to take steps to protect the trade of the Malaccan residents. They sent an extra yacht to Malacca to patrol against opium smuggling and piracy. Malacca was ordered to reestablish the outpost on the Dindings [Pulau Pangkor] off the coast of Perak to reinforce the patrolling vessels. The garrison was to consist of 25 to 30 European soldiers plus as many Malays but *no Bugis*. In these circumstances, the temptation to curb this Bugis menace may have outweighed, in Van Imhoff's mind, the desire to hold down costs. Though he never openly condoned an alliance with the Malay faction, he certainly did not stress the need for Malacca's neutrality in his correspondence with Governor Albinus.

Albinus was a resourceful and decisive man who took the Governor-General's instructions seriously and set out actively to seek ways to improve Malacca's trade, especially the tin trade. He had served in Malacca since 1738 as chief administrator, and so came to the post of governor in 1743 with a knowledge of local affairs. But he had not had direct experience of confrontations between Malacca and Johor, for the Dutch town had stayed determinedly neutral for over two decades. He began his task of re-invigorating Malacca's finances by sending expeditions to the Malay and Sumatran ports to buy tin and gold at the best possible price. He sent Ondercoopman Claas de Wind to the tin quarters to see what could be done to obtain better supplies of the mineral.[22] De Wind made a successful trip to Kedah, where he obtained 23,000 lbs of tin and a cargo of rice,[23] but this provided no permanent answer to

Malacca's dilemma, which was, as always, how to collect the amounts of tin the VOC needed at a price it was prepared to pay—invariably substantially lower than that paid by the Chinese, English, and other foreign merchants.

Albinus was well aware of the hostility between Malays and Bugis at the court of Johor. Against the current background of tension between Johor and the officials at Batavia (who had in the past tended to stop Malaccan initiatives aimed at weakening the Malay power), and ignoring the implication of the repeated instructions of the 1720s and 1730s to remain totally neutral in local quarrels, Albinus saw in the Malay-Bugis strife an opportunity to lead Malacca back to prosperity. He made overtures to the neighboring Malay princes. Lured as his predecessors of the previous century had been by the vision of substantial trading concessions for the VOC, Albinus let it be known that the Company no longer necessarily intended to remain aloof from local affairs. He was not reprimanded for this by Van Imhoff, or restrained in any way.

In February, 1745, Claas de Wind was sent from Malacca to Riau and Inderagiri. He carried letters from the Malacca government to the rulers of Johor with further complaints of the alleged piracies. He had been optimistically instructed by Albinus to persuade Sultan Sulaiman to deliver all the tin brought into Riau to the VOC and to exclude all foreign trade from the port in accordance with the terms of the treaty of 1713. Johor merchants were ordered to go in future to Malacca for provisions and to send all foreign vessels, especially Chinese junks, to Batavia. All tin from the Johor tin quarters was to be delivered to Malacca. Exactly how de Wind was to accomplish this "persuasion" was not explained in the written instructions; but it was specified that this was to be done by "mercantile" means, as it was "wholly inconvenient to the Company to meddle unnecessarily in any native differences" at that time.[24] So the prohibition against interference was technically enforced. But Albinus must have known that none of the objectives of the mission could be attained without offering at least some hope of a Dutch alliance with the Malays against the Bugis, and it is likely that de Wind had less cautious verbal instructions.

On 19 May 1745, while de Wind was probably still in Riau, the Bugis Raja Muda Daeng Cellak died. His successor, Daeng Kamboja, the son of Daeng Parani, was at that time in Selangor, and the Malay faction seems to have taken this opportunity to press their influence with Sulaiman. It is not my purpose here to pursue Johor domestic politics, except insofar as it influenced Dutch policies, but at this time the Malay faction made an attempt to capture the presence of the ruler, that most potent of Malay symbols, from the Bugis, who had controlled him since 1722. Sulaiman's own part in this is unclear. He appears to have kept faithfully to his bargain with the Bugis after his one abortive attempt to escape in July, 1723. The Malay leader of this attempt to expel the Bugis was Mansur Syah, and his tactics were obviously aimed at keeping the Bugis leaders away from Sulaiman. The Bugis author of the *Tuhfat-al Nafis* hints plainly at Bugis suspicions that Daeng Cellak was poisoned by Mansur Syah's faction,[25] and there is evidence from Dutch and Bugis sources of Malay attempts, led by the Trengganu prince, to rid the Riau court of the Bugis for good.[26] But the Malays lacked the strength to do this on their own, and turned again to their old allies, the Dutch.

A conciliatory letter was sent from Riau to Batavia, with the result that Claas de Wind was again despatched to Riau in February, 1746. Here he was met with fair words and promises that Sultan Sulaiman "in future would be dissuaded from all tyranny . . . [and] that the Malaccan inhabitants would be able to use this foreshore [Malacca] freely and without molestation." Sulaiman promised to prevent all piracy in the vicinity of Malacca. But even in this delicate approach, the Malays were mindful of their priorities. Sulaiman (or Mansur Syah) specifically refused to forbid foreign trading vessels to enter the port of Riau, or to promise to deliver all of the tin brought into Riau to the VOC, for this they knew would provoke the general hatred of the people of Riau, who relied on trade for a living. The Dutch still paid substantially less for tin than any of the other foreign merchants. But, to prove the sincerity of his desire for the friendship of the VOC despite these reservations, Sultan Sulaiman made the Company the princely gift of the Sumatran territory of Siak.[27]

Johor had not ruled in Siak since the rebellion of 1718, for the Siak leader Raja Kecik, though driven from the other Johor territories by the combined power of the Bugis and Sulaiman's remaining loyal Malay forces, had retained his control over this Sumatran territory. Siak was now ruled by Raja Kecik's son, Mahmud, who had continued his father's feud with the Riau Bugis, attacking Selangor in 1746. Raja

Mahmud was encouraging the visits of Indian merchants and also trading to Kedah, whose ruler, Muhammad Jiwa, imported his own supplies of cloth from India. Inland tin was sent to Kedah in exchange for these commodities.[28] As usual, the other foreign merchants could offer much more attractive rates than the Company or its dependents. English country traders were among those who visited Siak, particularly a Captain Munro who was a frequent caller. The foreigners brought opium as well as cloth, furnishing another problem for the Company. For the Javanese who brought rice, salt, and other provisions to the Sumatran port, bought the opium and carried it back to Java, circumventing the Company's efforts to secure a monopoly of the import of opium to Java. In 1746 Malaccan authorities felt obliged to go against their standing instructions and admit a vessel from Java which arrived without a Company pass "for fear he might go and deal with the English Captain Munro at Siak, and take opium and cloth back to Java."[29]

Wisely, perhaps, the Malaccan governor made no immediate attempt to act on this gift. Albinus was well aware that Sulaiman was not motivated solely by altruism in this matter; he was himself inclined to believe that Sulaiman had been persuaded to make this gift to the VOC in the hope of revenging himself on Raja Kecik's family, by involving them in conflict with the Dutch over the control of Siak.[30] Commercial motives may also have played a part in Sulaiman's decision. The attraction of foreign trade to Siak was not likely to have been viewed with any more favor by Sultan Sulaiman and Raja Muda Daeng Cellak of Johor than it was by Malacca. But the opportunity to gain sovereignty over Siak was not wholly unwelcome to the VOC, even if the motives behind the gift were suspect. Van Imhoff made no objection to Malacca's acceptance of Siak—it is perhaps another indication that he did not see the need for neutrality in Malay affairs as strongly as his predecessors had—and recommended that Malacca use Johor's gift as a "big stick" to regulate Siak's ruler when necessary: "Firstly it will be sufficient that you hold him steadily in fear and prevent him admitting any of our competitors even the Chinese junks and so that the small trade of the Malaccan inhabitants remains free and open and our rights to cut timber [are respected]."[31]

Siak had represented a thorny point in Malacca-Johor relations for nearly a century. Malacca had been on close terms, commercially, with Siak since the 1670s. In the 1740s the two places enjoyed a mutually beneficial trade which was, if anything, even more essential to Malacca's welfare than it had been when the Raja Muda of Johor tried to terminate it in 1710. Albinus certainly did not wish to see this traffic interrupted. The VOC and the Malacca freeburghers went to Siak to buy gold and timber supplies; the gold trade to Patupahan had been especially profitable lately, and even the cloth trade was improving.

Raja Mahmud of Siak was reputedly embittered by the gift, and declared that Siak and Riau were subject to the ruler of Pagar Ruyung, and that he would accept the authority of no other power.[32] But Albinus sent friendly letters, hoping to bring the prince to recognize the new rights of the VOC in Siak, including their right to free trade, by peaceful means.[33] He was reasonably successful in this. The gold and timber trade continued on a healthy basis, and some progress was also made in the cloth trade in conjunction with the gold trade. In 1749 Albinus noted that "the sale of the Company's cloth and other commodities forms the basis of the gold trade," though he continued with a warning that the success of that trade "depends on untiring effort in the face of numerous competitors."[34] The Company still found it hard to establish a market for the cloth and other goods they brought because of competition from other foreign merchants. But any benefits to be won by suppressing the foreign trade were felt to be minor in comparison with the costs this would entail. Once more Batavia was looking over its shoulder at the specter of financial loss.

Albinus also continued to search for ways of increasing Malacca's tin collection for the VOC. In 1746 a fresh contract was negotiated with the small state of Nanning,[35] and patrolling was used to stop the export of tin produced in Rembau, Nanning, and the other small states of Malacca's hinterland. Guardships were set at the entrances of the Panagi and Muar Rivers, but it was feared that the Malaccan government might be exceeding its authority by taking this action in Johor's territory and Batavia advised caution. They ordered that the patrols "were not to make the use of these rivers impossible to the hinterland people, but were only to make them bring tin down the Malacca river, and to prevent the carriage of this mineral to the English and others at Selangor." The patrols were not greatly effective, for Malacca, with a garrison of

364 at this time, could not police even this small area efficiently.[36] An appeal was made to Sultan Sulaiman to authorize the actions of his new ally, but he could give nothing but his verbal authority for the Bugis dominated the rivers.[37]

Another venture of Albinus' that involved cooperation with a Malay regime was, however, to put the Malaccan tin trade on a safe footing for decades to come. In 1746 he was able to re-open the VOC's outpost in Perak, shut down since 1690.[38] Perak was a major tin producing state. It had been attached to the Malacca Sultanate and later lost to Aceh. The VOC's experiences with Perak in the previous century had not been encouraging; so much so that when envoys from Perak visited Malacca in 1710 requesting that the Company's post be re-established, they were not welcomed. The government pointed out that the Perak ruler still owed the Company "the considerable sum of 43,430 rds" and that this must be repaid and other indications of good faith given before the Company could venture to trust Perak again.[39] Apparently Perak also had second thoughts, for the promised second mission to clarify these matters never materialized.[40] Alexander Hamilton, an English merchant familiar with the Straits in the early eighteenth century, wrote of Perak at that time that it "produces more tin than any [other place] in India, but the Inhabitants are so Treacherous, Faithless and Bloody, that no European Nation can keep Factories there with safety."[41] No record of further overtures by Perak to Malacca occur till the 1740s, when the combination of the renewed Dutch interest in the tin trade and mounting apprehension in the court of Perak at the increasing strength of their neighbors in Selangor were to give rise to a new, and more lasting, alliance between Malacca and Perak.

In early 1746, in accord with the new policy of actively pursuing trade urged by Van Imhoff, Albinus sent a mission to the ruler of Perak. The Malaccan government's letters to Batavia make it clear that Albinus had been encouraged to sound Perak out once again because of the political situation in the Straits. The Bugis had been intriguing with a faction of the Perak *orang kaya* to secure a monopoly of tin output; in 1743 they had openly attacked. The fragile independence of Perak's ruler was threatened by the growing commercial and strategic power of the Bugis, and Albinus felt he might welcome an ally even at the expense of a lower price for tin. Albinus therefore "gradually prepared the ground with Perak, and just at the time when the Buginese had worked out a division of the tin interests among the members of the court of that Kingdom, I obtained an exclusive contract through a special envoy."[42] This contract promised all Perak's tin to the VOC at a fixed price of Sp.$.34 per bahar [about 42 rds]. The old fort on Pangkor near the mouth of the Perak River was re-occupied. The Dutch garrison later moved upstream to Tanjung Putus where a stone fort was built.[43] The permission to build in stone was a marked favor to the Dutch, and signified a turning point in the history of their tin trade in the Straits of Malacca. When he left Malacca Albinus wrote:

> As a result of these arrangements I had the satisfaction last year of not only completely fulfilling the requirements of the Home Country and the Indies to the amount of 420,250 lbs (that is 200,250 lbs for the Netherlands, 200,000 lbs for China and 20,000 lbs for Surat) but also of being able to send 100,125 lbs to Batavia thus making a total of 520,375 lbs. Furthermore out of the residue at present available in the go-downs here and in Perak together with that which has been contracted for in the hinterlands, it will be easy to find the required amount for China which has been fixed at an amount equal to the annual shipment to Batavia.[44]

Albinus' success with the tin trade did not stand alone. At the end of his stint as Governor of Malacca the port's financial position had noticeably improved. For a time the gold trade flourished because Batavia allowed higher prices to be paid. In 1749 a quantity of gold dust was obtained from Patupahan and Inderagiri, and Batavia "strongly recommended that trade in that article should be maintained without interruption." These successes encouraged Albinus to argue that he had in fact turned Malacca into a "source of profit to the Company."[45] However, this was not accepted by Batavia, which replied that, "Although Your Excellency believes Malacca makes a profit from the tin and gold and is therefore no longer a *lastpost,* we can by no means accept this until the real profits make good the costs."[46] The VOC's system of keeping accounts clouds the issue, making it difficult to see just how Malacca stood in relation to other VOC holdings. The increasing revenue from the trade to China, which was to finally allow Malacca to pay its way in the 1760s, was undoubtedly already having a useful effect on the old port's income. With a couple of exceptions the official figures continued to show a loss until 1768,[47] but Albinus himself believed that he had placed the town firmly on the road to a more prosperous future.

One thing had clearly changed by the time Albinus left Malacca in 1749—the Company no longer stood aloof from its Malay neighbors, or their quarrels. The VOC had been drawn into the web of political intrigue which surrounded the Malay-Bugis court of Johor and its satellites. Interference in Perak and Siak had put the Dutch squarely in the path of Bugis ambitions in the Straits, a position they had assiduously avoided during the previous two decades. Albinus was himself cautious in his dealings with his new allies; though he was promised all the tin produced in the Johor territories if Malacca helped the Malays regain control of them, he only gave token support.[48] When, in 1747, Sulaiman attacked Raja Kecik's son Raja Alam of Siak on Siantan, the Malacca government sent gunpowder and provisions to Riau, but avoided any direct involvement in the fray.[49] However, the Dutch were not slow to give Sulaiman advice where the Bugis were concerned. In their first interview Albinus asked the Malay Sultan "why he did not first drive out the Buginese [by whose permission he appeared to rule,] from the Straits, and then bring the various peoples under his own authority?"[50] By skillful maneuvering of the situation, Albinus managed to maintain his position as an interested but uninvolved party. The next two governors, Pieter van Heemskerk and Willem Dekker, were to prove less skilled or less lucky in dealing with Malay ways, and were not so successful in balancing their new interests with Batavia's desire to avoid becoming too involved in local politics, especially in local wars.

Siak, always a vital area for Malacca's prosperity, and since the 1746 treaty nominally at least a Dutch territory, now became the cause of its deeper involvement in the Malay-Bugis dispute. When the old ruler Raja Kecik died in 1746,[51] he left two sons, Raja Mahmud and Raja Alam. Mahmud was the son of Kecik's royal wife, Tengku Kamariah of Johor. Raja Kecik lost his reason before he named his successor, and the battle over the succession threw Siak into grave disorder. Finally Raja Alam was driven out and retreated to Batu Bahara.

Soon afterwards Raja Kecik died, and Mahmud was installed as Sultan of Siak. Raja Alam then allied himself to the Bugis by marrying Daeng Kamboja's daughter, and, thus strengthened, in 1753 he drove his brother out of Siak and set himself up as ruler.[52] Raja Mahmud turned to his uncle, Sultan Sulaiman, for support. At this point the Siak problem became an added point of issue between the Malay and the Bugis factions.

Siak was now, nominally at least, a VOC possession. Batavia assured the Directors in 1754 that the Company would not be drawn into this affair, at least not openly,[53] but the Malaccan government was obviously disturbed by the effects of the constant skirmishing and piratical behavior of the warring factions on the local trade, including that of their own independent merchants.[54] A new treaty intended to safeguard this important Siak trade was even then being drawn up between the VOC and Sulaiman of Johor. The final draft of this treaty of 1754 was rejected by Malacca because Sulaiman inserted a clause pledging the VOC to help him against his rebellious subjects *whoever they may be*; a promise that proved far too sweeping for Dutch taste. An alternative draft was finally accepted in 1756.[55] Meanwhile, Siak remained a cause of concern to Malacca's governor, Willem Dekker. The acute disruption to Siak's trade which followed its capture by Raja Alam soon became so damaging that Malacca felt bound to act. A small force was sent to reinforce the Johorese in August, 1755 and Raja Alam was once more expelled from Siak.[56] But as the Directors had feared, this victory was only to lead to greater problems for Malacca.

The hostility between Malay and Bugis in Riau now became open, and the Bugis Raja Muda, Daeng Kamboja, left Riau (to which he had returned in 1748 despite Mansur, though his main base seems to have remained in Selangor) once more for Linggi, taking with him "all the canon, a good number of vessels and many people, mostly Bugis."[57] He was joined by Raja Alam, who was attempting to combine his Minangkabau followers and the Bugis against Sulaiman and the VOC.[58] The allies even wrote to Perak, attempting to woo the new Sultan, Iskandar, away from his alliance with Malacca.[59]

Faced with this hostile alliance and tempted by the possible advantages promised by the 1756 treaty "if the Bugis are brought under control," Dekker decided, perhaps rashly, to take direct action.[60] When Sulaiman visited Malacca with his forces early in 1756, the Governor suggested that they crush the Bugis "once and for all" with their combined forces. Sulaiman, always unwilling to definitely break his ties with the Bugis, was less eager for an immediate confrontation, pleading that he must return to protect his capital. The leader of the Malay faction opposing the Bugis, Mansur Syah, promised to return as soon as possible but, though "daily expected," did not reappear at Malacca till June, and then only to further delay the attack. In the meantime, Daeng Kamboja had seized the initiative and, supported by the forces of Raja Alam and Raja Hadil of Rembau, laid siege to Malacca. It was the first time the port had been under attack since 1641.

Malacca was besieged by the Bugis and Minangkabaus from October, 1756 till July, 1757. The fortress does not seem to have been in any real danger of capture by the Bugis, but its functions as a VOC outpost were greatly hampered, and its prestige in the Malay world was immeasurably damaged.[61] The Malacca hinterland was devastated and many of the inhabitants fled into the town, causing "much poverty and misery," and threatening a drastic reduction in Malacca's domestic income. The increased pressure on supplies underlined a grave weakness in Malacca's position; the lack of a local food supply. Food, especially rice, had always had to be imported, generally from Java, Siam, or Kedah. Now the ruler of Kedah, already hostile to Malacca because the latter's treaty with Perak had stopped up an important source of Kedah's tin imports, "absolutely refuses to sell his food to the Malay people who come here."[62]

Batavia was forced to intervene. By February, 1757, Malacca was requesting reinforcements and in June 80 European soldiers were sent from Bantam.[63] In March there was an abortive truce and negotiations with the Bugis leaders were begun. The Bugis demanded that the VOC relinquish its alliance with Sulaiman and withdraw from Siak, but Malacca refused to negotiate on this basis, as it felt this would leave the Bugis free to dominate the Straits to the detriment of the interests of the Company and the Malaccan residents.[64] It would also have involved an unacceptable loss of prestige for the Company. Negotiations were opened again in April but the Bugis demands had not altered and were again rejected. Malacca made counter demands that Daeng Kamboja submit to Sulaiman and give up control of the tin-places to him.

With the failure of these negotiations, the siege appears to have broken up; Daeng Kamboja withdrew to Linggi, where he was in turn attacked by Dutch forces, after the reinforcements from Batavia arrived. The Bugis did not care to enter serious hostilities with Batavia, and the war came to an end in January, 1758, when the Bugis formally submitted to the Company and new treaties were drawn up between the VOC and Daeng Kamboja, and the leaders of Selangor, Nanning and Rembau. These treaties confirmed the terms of the VOC–Johor Treaty of 1757; Linggi and Rembau were ceded to the VOC, which was to receive all their tin production, and no other foreign shipping was to be allowed to enter any of the ports of these places.[65] A Dutch outpost was established at Linggi to oversee these provisions.

So the first open trial of strength between the VOC and the Bugis ended in an apparent victory for the VOC, and an increase—at least on paper—in Malacca's territory. The Dutch had made valuable gains in Siak and in their relationship with Perak, and had withstood the combined strength of the Bugis; but the power of the Bugis remained essentially unbroken. The Company had been dragged into an expensive conflict, the very thing Batavia had for so long attempted to avoid; the inhabitants and freeburghers of Malacca had had to bear extreme hardship; and the Company's annual expenditure in Malacca had risen sharply.[66] Governor-General Jacob Mossel justified the affair to the Directors on the "irreproachable" grounds that Raja Alam had "wished to drive our ally [Mahmud] out of his kingdom, whereby the balance would have been very harmfully upset if the Company had not come to Siak's aid."[67] Despite this protestation, and the previously avowed determination of Batavia "not to abandon our Johoor ally,"[68] the VOC returned to the previous policy of strict neutrality in their Malacca dependency as soon as possible after the peace negotiations. They rejected Sulaiman's requests that they set up a post at Riau to protect his capital from the Bugis.[69] Though Malacca appeared to have made gains from its alliance with the Malays, Malacca's master in Batavia, no Van Imhoff (who had died in 1750) did not seem convinced that the gains were worth the costs.

The Bugis siege of Malacca in 1756–58 was not the result of a Bugis effort to drive the Dutch out of Malacca, or of a VOC plan to free Johor from the Bugis. Nor had the Dutch Company officially ever reversed its stated policy of neutrality in the Straits. Governor-General Van Imhoff, in his zeal to revitalize the VOC's waning prosperity, had merely relaxed Batavia's normally stringent requirement that Malacca maintain a policy of strict neutrality in the affairs of the Straits; and Governor

Albinus of Malacca, caught between Batavia's demands for increased profitability and its continuing unrealistic restrictions on trade, had seized on this relaxation "to fish in the troubled waters" of the Malay Bugis quarrel to win trade concessions for Malacca. Van Imhoff's day had come and gone, and with it Malacca's brief period of freedom to use Malay politics for its own ends. The results had been much as the earlier Batavian governments had predicted.

NOTES

1. The strength of Batavia's resolve not to allow Malacca to re-emerge as a major port can be seen in the 1780s when Malaccan governors de Bruijn and Couperus pleaded for a chance to implement some reasonable commercial policies at Malacca to attract the trade driven out of Riau. Such pleas fell on deaf ears in Batavia, which was arguably more wary of a revitalized Malacca than of the Bugis. See Brian Harrison, "Trade in the Straits of Malacca in 1785," *JMBRAS*, 26:1 (1953): 56–62. J. de Hullu, "A. E. Van Braam Houckgeest's Memorie over Malakka en den Tinhandel aldaar (1790)," *BKI* 76 (1920): 284–309, and de Hullu, "De Engelschen op Poeloe Pinang en de Tinhandel der Oost-Indische Compangie (VOC) in 1788," *BKI*, 77 (1921): 605–14.

2. L. Andaya notes the disarray among the *orang laut* and their unwillingness to support Sulaiman against Raja Kecik in his *Kingdom of Johor*, 304, 306ff.

3. These were called "country traders." See Holden Furber, *John Company at Work—A Study of European Expansion in India in the Late 18th Century.*

4. This is corroborated by the Malaccan Shipping Lists [Boomboeken] for the century. The lists are located in the annual Overgekomende Brievenboeken of the VOC at the Rijksarchief, The Hague.

5. Glamann, *Dutch-Asiatic Trade*, 248–29.

6. J. E. Heeres, "De 'Consideratien' van Van Imhoff," *BKI*, 66 (1912): 441–621.

7. Hall, *History of South East Asia*, 334.

8. Kol. Arch. 2542, Report on Malacca, Malacca to Batavia (22 October 1745): 1426–531.

9. Kol. Arch. 2506, Generale Missiven (26 October 1744): 121. My italics.

10. van der Chijs, *Realia*, 2: 178.

11. Batavia to Malacca, (12 November 1745): 714.

12. van der Chijs, *Realia*, 2: 181-82.

13. Kol. Arch. 2528, Generale Missiven (31 December 1745): 520.

14. Kol. Arch. 2567, Malacca to Batavia (23 February 1746): 59.

15. The de facto ruler of Malacca had often been one of the great nobles; the Laksamana of the 1680s or the Bendahara of the time of the Sultan Mahmud

who was defeated by the Portuguese, but I have found no record of a powerful Raja Muda prior to 1708; the rank is defined by Wilkinson as that given to the heir-apparent. Wilkinson, *Dictionary*, 192.

16. Kol. Arch. 1893, Generale Missiven (30 November 1724): 847.

17. B. Andaya, "An Examination of the Sources concerning the Reign of Sultan Mansur Shah of Trengganu, 1741–1793," JMBRAS 49.2 (1976): 80–106.

18. Kol. Arch. 2483, Generale Missiven (5 April 1743): 24

19. Raja Ali Haji ibn Ahmad, *The Precious Gift*, 90.

20. Batavia to Malacca (17 July 1744): 594–97.

21. Kol. Arch. 2542, Malacca to Batavia (29 December, 1744): 1–6. This is a Dutch version of a letter from the Sultan of Johor to Governor-General Van Imhoff.

22. van der Chijs, *Realia* 2: 181.

23. Kol. Arch. 2522, Malacca to Batavia (30 April 1744): 624.

24. Kol. Arch. 2542, Malacca to Batavia (6 February 1745): 71–74.

25. Netscher, *Djohor*, 71. Governor Albinus mentions this rumor. The author of the *Tuhfat* mentions a "disordered" person who came to Riau at this time "acting in a manner which violated Malay custom and tradition"—and then immediately goes on to say that Mansur Syah arrived in Riau six days before Daeng Cellak suddenly died. He concludes: "Please reflect on the significance of what has just been said." Raja Ali Haji ibn Ahmad, *The Precious Gift*, 92.

26. Raja Ali Haji ibn Ahmad, *The Precious Gift*, 93ff.

27. Kol. Arch. 2542, Malacca to Batavia (23 February 1746): 44, 115, and Kol. Arch. 2549, Generale Missiven, (31 December 1746): 285. See also Brian Harrison, "Malacca in the 18th century: two Dutch Governors' Reports," *JMBRAS* 27.1 (1954): 25.

28. D. N. Lewis, "Kedah; the Development of a Malay State," in Reid and Castles, 36–43.

29. Kol. Arch. 2567, Malacca to Batavia (6 November 1746): 463.

30. Kol. Arch. 2592, Malacca to Batavia (1 April 1747): 434.

31. Batavia to Malacca (22 October 1746): 690.

32. Kol. Arch. 2576, Generale Missiven (31 December 1747): 308.

33. Kol. Arch. 2592, Malacca to Batavia (9 January 1747): 20..

34. Cited in Harrison, "Malacca in the 18th century," 28. The area remained a sensitive one to which Malaccan governors took care to cater. See Kol. Arch. 2858, Malacca to Batavia (10 March 1759): 189, Governor Dekker's Memorie (1758).

35. J. E. Heeres and F. W. Stapel, *Corpus Diplomaticum Neerlando-Indicum, 1596–1799*, 5: 426–30.

36. Kol. Arch. 2576, Generale Missiven (31 December 1747): 310.

37. Kol. Arch. 2592, Malacca to Batavia (9 January 1747): 15.

38. B. Andaya, *Perak*, 50–51.

39. Batavia to Malacca (11 July 1710): 734.

40. Ibid. 53.

41. Hamilton, *A New Account,* 2: 40. Hamilton is not always reliable, for his prejudices often lead him astray.

42. Cited in Harrison, "Malacca in the 18th century," 26. Governor Albinus' Memorandum, 15 February 1750.

43. Kol. Arch. 2567, Malacca to Batavia (18 August 1746): 418.

44. Cited in Harrison, "Malacca in the 18th century," 26–27. Governor Albinus' Memorandum, 15 February 1750.

45. Cited in Harrison, "Malacca in the 18th century," 29. Governor Albinus' Memorandum, 15 February 1750.

46. Batavia to Malacca (7 January 1751): 717.

47. See Appendix II.

48. Harrison, "Malacca in the 18th century," 25. Governor Albinus' Memorandum, 15 February 1750.

49. Kol. Arch. 2592, Malacca to Batavia (24 May 1747): 453.

50. Cited in Harrison, "Malacca in the 18th century," 25. Governor Albinus' Memorandum, 15 February 1750.

51. Netscher, *Djohor,* 77.

52. Kol. Arch. 2700, Generale Missiven (31 December 1753): 454.

53. Kol. Arch. 2719, Generale Missiven (31 December 1754): 559. Malacca claimed never to have promised aid to Sulaiman. Kol. Arch. 2712, Malacca to Batavia (17 March 1753): 167.

54. Kol. Arch. 2753, Malacca to Batavia (30 April 1755): 53.

55. Netscher, *Djohor,* 81–85.

56. Kol. Arch. 2753, Malacca to Batavia (31 August 1755): 317.

57. Raja Ali Haji ibn Ahmad, *The Precious Gift,* 104.

58. Kol. Arch. 2753, Malacca to Batavia (27 September 1755): 327–28.

59. B. Andaya, *Perak,* 138.

60. Kol. Arch. 2776, Malacca to Batavia (9 April 1756): 33.

61. Netscher, *Djohor,* 91.

62. Kol. Arch. 2753, (Captain Gerrit Zeeman's Report on Kedah, 19 June 1755): 23.

63. Kol. Arch. 2776, Malacca to Batavia (4 February 1757): 20. Batavia to Malacca (7 June 1757): 20.

64. Kol. Arch. 2801, Malacca to Batavia (26 August 1757): 18–23.

65. Heeres and Stapel, *Corpus Diplomaticum,* 6: 148–49. See also Kol. Arch. 2827, Malacca to Batavia (6 February 1758): 15.

66. See Netscher, "Twee Belegeringen van Malakka, (1756/7 en 1784)," 310, for the sufferings of the people of Malacca. This is an excerpt from the since lost *Malacca Daghregister* [Malacca's Diary] for the period of the siege.

67. Kol. Arch. 2786, Note by Governor-General Jacob Mossel about Malacca (13 April 1758): 1459.

68. Kol. Arch. 2783, Generale Missiven (31 December 1757): 648.

69. Kol. Arch. 2827, Malacca to Batavia (6 February 1758): 19.

5

NEUTRALITY
REVISITED

It soon became evident that the VOC's new treaties with Johor and Linggi were only as good as the Company's ability to enforce them. In direct contravention of the treaties, the Malay and Bugis ports of Riau, Selangor, Kedah and Trengganu admitted ever increasing numbers of foreign, especially English, ships, after 1758. With the ink hardly dry on his treaty with the VOC the ruler of Selangor allowed an English merchant to discharge a cargo of opium in his port in exchange for tin.[1] By the time of Daeng Kamboja's death in 1777 Riau had once again become "the *rendezvous* of the private trade here in the Straits," a meeting place for merchants and merchandise from all corners of the Archipelago and beyond.[2] And neither Batavia nor Malacca made any attempt to combat this state of affairs.

Batavia certainly had good reason to revert to its former policy of complete neutrality. The siege of Malacca in 1757–58 and its aftermath were sharp lessons in the expensive consequences of Dutch involvement in the affairs of Malacca's neighbors. Even in alliance with the Malays, the VOC in its depleted late eighteenth century state could no longer afford to field the necessary men and munitions to drive the Bugis from the Straits. If such action had been possible, there would have been no guarantee that Malacca would have profited; in the century of their dealings with the Malay princes the VOC had not found them notably docile or uncompetitive.[3] During the recent conflict, Malacca's Malay allies had been prepared only to make concessions in those areas which were of no interest to them personally; even the Malay leader who had urged the Malacca officials into open conflict with the Bugis, Mansur Syah of Trengganu, conceded remarkably little in return. In Siak, Raja Mahmud had been restored to power by Dutch forces, but rather than acquiesce with Dutch trade restrictions, turned openly against the Company. Perak also appeared to be an unstable ally, ready to break off relations with the VOC when the Bugis besieged Malacca, and constantly in the grip of faction fights. It is not surprising that Batavia, having rescued Malacca at considerable expense in 1758, then firmly enforced the policy of non-interference in the affairs of the Straits area. Malacca withdrew completely from the Malay-Bugis struggle in Johor after 1758—there is no indication that they offered even clandestine help to the Malay faction after that date.

The paradox of this period is that Malacca also seemed content to abide by the policy of neutrality. The key to this lay in a sudden about-face in Malacca's financial situation, and the escape of the port from its century-old classification by the VOC administration as a *lastpost,* a cost-heavy, inefficient establishment that was unable to pay its own way and constituted a drain on the Company's over-all finances. For, though the VOC had been forced virtually to drop out of the pepper, cloth, and gold trades, and though a Malaccan Governor could write that "the sale of goods is at present reduced to nothing, with no indication that any improvement may be fairly anticipated,"[4] the increase of shipping through the Straits was such that Malacca's income from the collection of port duties began to more than cover its expenses.[5] For most of the first five decades of the eighteenth century, an average of only thirty foreign ships called at Malacca each year; in the 1760s that number more than doubled. The increasing through-trade consisted mainly of China- or Manila-bound vessels which called at Malacca for supplies rather than cargo, though occasionally the Company was willing to sell spices to such inter-Asian trade, especially to the Manila-bound vessels. The increasing financial dependence of Malacca on the harbor dues generated by this traffic underlined the need for peace and security in the Straits, making Malacca's interests in the Straits coincide, for once, with Batavia's.

Malacca and Batavia certainly concurred in the need to remain aloof from further Malay-Bugis quarrels in the Straits. They were aided in this by the Bugis leader himself. Daeng Kamboja smoothed Malacca's path to neutrality by carefully maintaining good relations with the Dutch; he appeared content with his control of Riau, and made no move to enlarge his territories or revive the old hegemony of Johor in the Straits. Nor did he attempt to challenge the VOC's new status in Siak, or to come openly between Malacca and Perak. On the contrary, he cultivated friendly personal relations with VOC employees at Malacca.[6] He had no more desire than Batavia for further direct confrontation; his siege of Malacca had proved not only futile, but unnecessary. The needs of the new trade were best served by peace, which confrontation with the Dutch could only endanger. However, he could not resist—probably would have thought it politically unwise to resist—flirting with the English, his most profitable customers; in 1769 he reportedly invited the merchant Francis Light to establish a factory on Pulau Besong, near Bintan, "for the convenience of carrying on trade with the English."[7]

By 1770 Malacca faced a much rosier future than anyone could have predicted twenty or thirty years earlier. Though the VOC kept out of Malay-Bugis rivalry in Johor after 1758, they did not abandon the positive gains made by Governor Albinus in the 1740s; the treaty with Perak, and the cession of Siak to the Company by Sultan Sulaiman. These were directly tied to two of the constant problems of Malaccan trade, the assurance of continued access to Siak, important in the gold trade and for Malacca's freeburghers, and the power to obtain annually the required amount of tin. The importance of Siak to Malacca had not diminished with the years, and the Siak trade had been one of the incentives used by the Malays to draw Malacca from its neutrality in the previous decade. Malacca found their problems with Siak had not disappeared after Johor handed them the overlordship of the territory. The ruler of Siak, Raja Mahmud, son of Raja Kecik and his Johor wife, Tengku Kamariah,[8] was not content to be a vassal of the Dutch, though he had been returned to power by their agency. He had shown little inclination to come to Malacca's aid in 1757. The Dutch had consequently placed severe restrictions on trade to the Siak River; the entry of any vessels from the west, including Aceh, Kedah, and any port in India, was prohibited.[9] By this means the Company hoped to keep control of the valuable gold and cloth trade to the Minangkabau hinterlands. A Dutch garrison was quartered on Pulau Gontong in the mouth of the Siak River, and Company guardships patrolled the area.[10] By 1758 these restrictions drove Raja Mahmud to turn openly to piracy to enhance his income.[11] The Dutch at Malacca were alarmed, but before they could move to curb his activities, Mahmud made a surprise attack on the Dutch post at Pulau Gontong and massacred the garrison.[12]

Such a flagrant challenge to the Company could not be allowed to go unpunished if the Dutch wished to maintain any presence in the Straits. But Malacca could not expel Mahmud without replacing him, so it hastily made peace with his brother, Raja Alam (a Bugis ally whose reputation among the Dutch was scarcely better than Raja Mahmud's). A treaty was signed with Raja Alam in January 1761,[14] and the new allies drove Raja Mahmud's son, Raja Ismail, from Siak, (Mahmud having in the meantime died). Relations between Siak and Malacca became peaceful once more, and remained so for the rest of the century, though Malacca certainly did not always have things all its own way in its dealings with its Sumatran vassal. Raja Alam had all his brother's pride, and was prepared to defy the VOC when it really mattered to him; he installed his son, Raja Muhammed Ali, as ruler of Siak without the prior approval of the VOC stipulated in the 1761 treaty,[15] he invaded Patupahan, the tin producing region on the upper reaches of the Siak River, and "hindered trade with the inland people" from upriver, and he disputed the amount of duty payable at Siak by Malacca merchants.[16] But, having spent much of his life in exile, he was more subtle in his dealings with the Dutch, avoiding the open confrontation which had forced the VOC to act against his brother, and Malacca, though often irritated by the Siak prince, did not find his activities sufficiently threatening to the Company's interests to try to arouse Batavia to any action. So the VOC was able to rule its new province with a light hand, though it continued to do its best to cut off direct trade between Siak and Java, or the ports to the west of Malacca. In 1765, the garrison at Pulau Gontong was withdrawn because Batavia considered its upkeep too expensive.[17] Fear of the growing power of the Bugis state centered at Riau, and perhaps a very human desire not to have to "go on his travels" again, was more effective in binding Raja Alam to the VOC than any Dutch garrison could have been.

When Raja Alam's son Muhammed Ali succeeded him as ruler of Siak in 1766, he was at first viewed with suspicion by the Company, because he declared his accession to the throne without first seeking the VOC's consent, but subsequently he was careful to be seen to respect Dutch interests, and to be "well disposed to the Company," to the extent that the Malaccan governor, Crans, wrote in 1777; "[Muhammad Ali] favors the Malaccan inhabitants that go there to trade as much as is in his power, without supporting himself entirely by smuggling as others do, or allowing it; a prince such as he has not ruled in a long time."[18] This cooperative attitude was notable in a world increasingly dominated by the Bugis ports of Riau and Selangor. Governor Crans went so far as to urge the Batavian authorities to relax the restrictions which had been placed on the trade between Siak and Java,[19] so that Muhammad Ali might be allowed to send not two but six vessels annually to Java, since, according to the Siak ruler, these vessels were "only sent to fetch rice and salt."[20]

But Crans was not willing to help Muhammad Ali in matters outside the commercial arena. In 1774 Raja Ismail, son of the exiled (and deceased) Raja Mahmud, and Muhammed Ali's cousin, made a bid to re-capture Siak. Ismail had allied himself with the disgruntled Malay chiefs, spending several years in Trengganu with Mansur Syah after his family was driven from Siak in 1761. After the failure of his attack on Siak, Ismail established himself on the Rokan River, much too close for Muhammad Ali's comfort. The latter applied to Malacca for help to "dislodge" this troublesome neighbor, but Crans decided politically that it was better to leave things as they were, as "it is to be hoped that the fears of the one regarding the other will force them both to act peacefully and shall oblige their further attachment to the Company."[21] This was an inter-Malay squabble from which the Bugis showed no signs of profiting. Indeed, when Ismail finally defeated his cousin in 1777, he was lenient with the defeated prince and showed himself willing to continue to cooperate with Malacca. Only in this way could he ensure any commercial future for Siak, as the Bugis grew increasingly powerful in the Straits.

For the immediate result of the Company's return to neutrality in 1758 had been a sweeping victory for the Bugis in the struggle for the control of Johor. Mansur Syah, the Trengganu prince who had led the anti-Bugis faction in Riau during the 1740s and 1750s, was so alarmed at the course events had taken after the 1758 treaty that he begged the Dutch to send a cruiser to patrol the foreshores of Riau and defend it from the Bugis, reporting that Sultan Sulaiman of Johor (who had called on Bugis assistance to win his throne in 1722) was in "great fear" of their return.[22] Without Dutch support, the Malay faction at Riau was not in a position to resist the Bugis. At the end of 1759, having waited three months for some sign of continuing support from the VOC, Mansur abandoned Riau and Sulaiman, withdrawing with his followers to Trengganu.[23] He had attempted to take Sultan Sulaiman and his family with him, a move which, if successful, would have weakened the Bugis considerably by depriving them of the legitimizing influence of the ruler. However, Sulaiman would not leave Riau, and this loss of control of the person of the Sultan constituted a severe handicap to Mansur's future role in Johor's internal power struggle.[24]

Since the Bugis had mostly withdrawn to Selangor in 1745 Riau had been underpopulated, and with this departure of the Trengganu Malays, in 1759, the port was reputedly quite "bare of folk," and could not hope to defend itself.[25] Economically the situation was even worse, for there was no trade, and rice and other staples had become expensive. Sulaiman had no real choice but to recall his old allies, the Bugis. A fleet led by Sulaiman's son, the Raja di Baruh Raja Abd al-Jalil, who seems not to have been as hostile to the Bugis as many of the other Malay *orang kaya*—he had married Tenkgu Putih, the daughter of the Raja Muda Daeng Cellak, and was brother-in-law to the renowned Bugis warrior-leader Raja Haji—was sent to fetch the Raja Muda Daeng Kamboja from the Bugis stronghold back to Riau. Significantly, "No princes accompanied him, only the Malay captains and sea-people."[26]

Meanwhile, a Bugis fleet led by Daeng Kamboja's nephew, Raja Haji, arrived in Riau. Tension ran high between Malay and Bugis. Then Sultan Sulaiman died (20 August 1760);[27] and news came that his son, the Raja di Baruh, had also died shortly after him, at Selangor. In these circumstances Daeng Kamboja returned to Riau and installed Sulaiman's eight-year-old grandson, Ahmad, on the throne of Johor, with himself as regent.[28]

The Bugis faction had thus regained control of the Sultanate practically without a struggle, and Daeng Kemboja soon illustrated the solidity of his power. The young Sultan Ahmad, Sulaiman's grandson, himself died shortly after his installation, and attempts by the Malay faction to force the selection of adult Sultan were swiftly and forcibly defeated. Daeng Kamboja then engineered the election of Ahmad's infant brother, Raja Mahmud, his armed Bugis overawing the Bendahara, Temenggung, and other Malays.[29] A subsequent plot by the Malay *orang kaya* and Ismail of Siak to attack Riau and remove the infant ruler to safety was also forestalled by the Bugis.[30] The Malay leaders, further weakened by Dutch attempts to collect the debts incurred by Sulaiman in the war (the Regent, Daeng Kamboja, now controlled Johor's wealth), abandoned open confrontation, the *orang kaya besar* withdrawing to territorial bases on the mainland from whence they continued their intrigues with little palpable success. Riau was left in the hands of Daeng Kamboja, who "brought peace to Riau and lived contentedly for some time."[31]

The Bugis port of Riau soon became the favored stopover of the growing English country trade between India and China. The Dutch expected little else.[32] The natural advantages of Riau were now reinforced by the widespread trading network set up by the Bugis within the Archipelago. Pepper and tin, the two most useful items in the trade to China; gold, jungle products of all kinds, rice and other foodstuffs, opium and cloth from India, even spices from the Moluccas, were available at the Bugis port. The Bugis traded where they wished, carrying products from areas to which the Dutch considered they had exclusive rights (such as tin from the island of Bangka, off the Sumatran coast), and selling them in Riau or Selangor to foreign merchants (whom they had contracted, in their treaties with the VOC, to keep out of their ports). Little, if any, effort was made by the VOC to curb this trade. The Bugis even brought cloth and opium to the ports of northern Java in exchange for foodstuffs, though the Batavian government had always been most anxious to control the distribution of these items within Java. The VOC took no consistent preventative action, apart from such steps as ordering in 1761 that all goods brought to Batavia, Java's east coast, or Cheribon, from "any place in the Straits of Malacca except Malacca itself" were to be charged double duty.[33] If this affected the trade between Riau and Java, it was not in any lasting way, for in March, 1774, Batavia was forced to strengthen the order, this time directly prohibiting trade between Johor and Java.[34] In April 1774, "taking into consideration that the Johorese might be able to pretend that the lack of opportunity to obtain the necessary supplies provided the authority for them to overcome their need by piracy," Batavia softened the ruling, deciding to allow Daeng Kamboja to send five ships annually to Semarang, to fetch rice and other necessary supplies.[35] In January, 1775, this prohibition was completely rescinded, because the authorities at Semarang had reported a significant decline in the small trade coming there, and a subsequent decline in the Company's income from tolls.[36]

Once more Riau had become the major entrepôt of the Straits. But times had changed, and Daeng Kamboja did not, like the last Malay Raja Muda Mahmud in 1708–18, try to suppress all other ports in the territories of Johor and force all trade to Riau. This Riau was not to be the center of a Malay-style Johor Empire—the Bugis were more independently-minded, and tended to pursue their own commercial ends unless their group as a whole came under attack. As a result, Riau was not the sole port to flourish during this new period of prosperity. The old port of Kedah and the new ports of Selangor and Trengganu, even Malacca itself, flourished in the new climate of expanding trade. Malacca's authorities objected, as usual, to the growing trade at these ports—especially the trade of the English—but made no move to suppress it. The treaties of 1758 were, as we have seen, dead letters almost as soon as they were signed. In 1759, Malacca tentatively suggested a Company outpost be established at Selangor to put a stop to the rapid growth of that port's "smuggling trade," for it could not be controlled with guardships alone.[37] But the plan would have been difficult and expensive to implement, and ran counter to Batavia's policy of contracting rather than expanding its commitments in the Straits. Indeed, even the post at Linggi, which had been set up after the 1758 siege of Malacca, was disbanded in 1759, largely on the grounds of expense.[38]

In the following two decades, Selangor's trade flourished as the Bugis made spices as well as tin available at the peninsular port. The Dutch made very little effort to curtail even this trade, though it was operating virtually on their doorstep. Protests were made, but Malacca spoke with a very weak voice in relation to most of the powers in the Straits, especially the Bugis, after 1758. In 1765, for instance, Malacca reported that the Sultan of Selangor had allowed the fleet of a notorious pirate to shelter in his river after attacking a VOC ship. Malacca wrote to Selangor claiming full reparations for the loss of the ship and its cargo, the return of the two Europeans who had been carried off, and the surrender of the chief offender to Dutch punishment. Governor Crans confided to Batavia that "this complaint is not really in proportion to the great size of the crime," but admitted that he was unable to deal with Selangor as firmly as he would have liked because he lacked the necessary forces.[39] Even this modest protest met with a rebuff; the Bugis leader of Selangor, Raja Lumu, replied unrepentantly that "he had greatly desired the presence of a Company ship" when the pirates were in his river, but had been unable to act against them without such support— underlining Malacca's weakness, and his own awareness of it.[40] Ships bound for Selangor from the south sailed daily past Malacca without stopping for the passes stipulated by the sixth article of Selangor's 1758 contract with the VOC. Governor Jan Crans wrote on the eve of his retirement in 1777, "Selangor is most injurious to the Company, on account of the frequent trade there of the English in particular, who mostly take tin."[41]

Malacca was also well aware of the expanding trade at the nearby ports of Kedah and Trengganu. Selangor was a new port, a product of the recent explosion of trade. Kedah was a very old port, older than Malacca by many centuries, and, though efforts had been made to bring it into the VOC's sphere of influence in the middle of the previous century, Kedah was by now well outside the Company's control. Kedah's prosperity fluctuated with the strength of its more powerful neighbors, and for much of the eighteenth century the disruption of Johor in the south and Siam in the north (in the wake of disastrous wars with Burma) gave Kedah the chance to take advantage of the increased flow of trade. Civil war in the 1720s caused a brief setback, but as the European trade from India increased, Kedah flourished. By 1750 its ruler, Raja Muhammad Jiwa, had begun to send ships to India; in 1759, one of these was seized by agents of the English East India Company at Madras as payment for an outstanding debt.[42] Some of Muhammad Jiwa's other ventures were more successful.[43] Kedah was the only significant rice-producing area in the Straits, and the chance to obtain fresh provisions attracted many of the growing number of merchants en route to China. The main cause of friction between Kedah and Malacca was Perak's tin—Muhammad Jiwa looked with a jaundiced eye on Malacca's association with Perak, as it swallowed up the greater portion Perak's tin production. In retaliation, Malaccan agents had not been permitted to purchase rice and other foodstuffs at Kedah, except for immediate use, throughout the 1750s.[44] Throughout the siege of Malacca this prohibition was extended to Malays bound for the Dutch port. The Malaccan government in turn suspected that much tin they felt to be rightfully theirs was disappearing from Perak via the inland route and down the Kedah River. They also feared, and not without cause, that Perak would be lured away from the Company by Muhammad Jiwa's constant pressure and intrigues in the Perak court. (He had even promised to dispose of all the elephants Perak wished to sell each year, if his neighbor would only deliver all its tin production to him.)[45] But Malacca could do nothing directly to prevent this threat to one of its most important assets. Indeed, in 1761 they attempted to placate Kedah by allowing Chinese junks to pass Malacca to visit the northern port.[46]

In the middle of the century merchants began finding their way to Trengganu, on the East Coast of the Peninsula. Trengganu, though somewhat deficient as a safe haven, situated as it was on the exposed east coast, was conveniently placed for the trade to China, and produced a flourishing pepper crop.[47] Pepper was growing in value as an import to China to use in exchange for the purchase of Chinese products, which had begun to be very profitable in Europe, and the VOC was having difficulties collecting suitable amounts from its previous suppliers in Malabar.[48] This combination of events stimulated Dutch interest in Trengganu's pepper. In 1758, VOC agents attempted to persuade Trengganu's ruler, their ally Mansur Syah, to deliver all the pepper produced in Trengganu to the Company. But Mansur avoided any commitment, claiming he had no control over the pepper trade.[49] By 1760, Malacca had decided to send no more missions directly to Trengganu, as the local price for pepper had risen beyond the amount they were authorized to pay. In 1762, pepper was selling to China–bound merchants for the (in VOC eyes) "excessive" price of Sp $12 per picul.[50]

Trengganu also attracted Chinese trade. Very few Chinese vessels had come to Malacca in the first half of the eighteenth century, but as the volume of trade increased after 1760, Chinese shipping began to reappear there.[51] Batavia aimed to attract all the Chinese trade to the Archipelago to itself. In 1765 they renewed the prohibition on all trade between Malacca and China, because "allowing the Chinese junks to trade at Malacca is prejudicial to the trade of Batavia."[52] The prohibition profited Trengganu as much as or more than Batavia; in 1766 Batavia commented on the frequent trade of the Chinese to the Malay state.[53] Malacca found this particularly irksome, but despite this, in January, 1774, permission was granted for vessels from Trengganu to trade to Batavia,[54] and the prohibition on Chinese trade to Malacca was renewed.[55] In 1779 a further ban brought forth heated protests from Malacca's freeburghers, who claimed that this regulation, if enforced, would only damage Malacca without benefitting Batavia, "because junks prohibited Malacca will only go to Trengganu."[56] But as usual such protests fell on deaf ears.

But overall Malacca continued to prosper. Despite Daeng Kamboja's apparent peaceful intentions, suspicion of the Bugis was strong among the Malays. It led the rulers of Perak to continue their alliance with Malacca in the 1760s and 1770s, and in the 1760s Malacca's tin trade throve as never before, despite the increasing number of foreign merchants calling at the Malay ports for the mineral. Malaccan supplies now came mainly from Perak, and though the rulers of both Bugis Selangor and Kedah continually intrigued in the court of Perak to break up this alliance, neither succeeded. The rulers of Perak continued to believe— probably rightly—that only by maintaining their link with the neutral port of Malacca could Perak maintain any measure of independence. Even though Malacca had lost much prestige in the Straits since the siege of 1757–58, the VOC remained a force to be reckoned with, and the port of Malacca, though weak in itself, had not been abandoned by the Company. Moreover, in the same way that the very existence of a neutral port had helped the Bugis when they were a minority struggling to evade the dominance of Raja Muda Mahmud, Malacca now allowed Perak to avoid the consequences of growing Bugis commercial power. Tin was Perak's main product, and main source of income. Without the contract with Malacca Perak would have been forced to sell its tin to the Bugis, or would have become a bone of contention between the rapidly expanding Bugis power and Kedah. Relations between the Dutch and Perak were not always serene, but no open break occurred in the 1760s or 1770s. The main disagreements centered on the Dutch payment for the tin, for Perak demanded payment in Spanish silver dollars, still the most widely acceptable currency in the Archipelago, and the VOC preferred to use its own Rijksdollars, which it could obtain more cheaply and easily. Eventually a compromise was reached, Perak agreed to accept Indian silver rupees, more accessible to the VOC, as well as Spanish dollars for its tin, and so the matter was resolved.[57]

It seemed that finally a modus vivendi had been reached between the Dutch and local communities in the Straits. Malacca and Batavia were now prepared to tolerate the Bugis entrepôt at Riau as long as it did not interfere with their vital contacts with Siak and Perak; and the Bugis seemed content to enjoy the growing international trade of Riau and their own inter-archipelagan trade and renounce that hegemony of the Straits which had been the goal of all previous dominant Malay ports. The Bugis empire was different from the old Malaccan and Johor empires, based as it was on the voluminous European country trade rather than the Chinese trade, allowing the Malay states freedom to sell their products to the Dutch port of Malacca and enjoy the prosperity which had come with the growing country trade. The Bugis had adapted the old Malay political blueprint to counter the disruption caused by the presence of a neutral but unassailable port within the Straits. Their compromise might well have worked, but for the Europeans themselves. But after a century of treating the Straits as a minor area where little profit was to be won, the Dutch were suddenly forced into an entirely different point of view, not by the Bugis, but by their fear of their old competitors, the English.

The growing trade through the Straits of Malacca had brought the Dutch a solution to their dilemma of financing the port without endangering Batavia's trade. It brought them also a new problem, which was to loom increasingly large in Batavia's thinking after 1770. Batavia's old fear that the English East India Company would attempt to renew its contact with the Archipelago had come much closer to reality in the 1760s and 1770s. As the English Company's trade to China grew, so did its need for the products of the Archipelago. The exchange problems faced by the English Company in their trade to China were only partially solved by the receipts of the growing country trade, and in the second half of the eighteenth century the Court of Directors in London began to consider seriously the establishment of a British settlement in the China Sea or the Malay Archipelago, where products acceptable on the China market could be obtained advantageously by the Company.[58] It was also hoped that Chinese junks would be drawn to such a port, and an Anglo-Chinese trade would emerge free of the difficulties and interference which plagued the English trade in Canton. By the 1760s the search for such an entrepôt had led to the temporary capture of Manila, and the unsuccessful settlement at Balambangan in the Sulu Archipelago, both places well outside the Dutch sphere of influence. The following decade saw the failure of these schemes. The growing urgency of the English Company's payment problem in China, and, perhaps, the obvious inability of the VOC to curb the growing Bugis and Malay ports in the Straits, opened the door to a different approach, and official English missions were sent to negotiate possible settlements at Aceh and Kedah.

The Dutch were well aware of this increased English activity and fearful of its implications. In 1769 they speculated that Daeng Kamboja and the Sultan of Selangor might draw on English help for their war with Kedah.[60] But the English Company was unable to come to terms with either Kedah or Aceh because they were prepared to offer too little and required too much in return. As unwilling as their rivals the Dutch to be drawn into the endless Malay-Bugis controversies, they refused to join with Muhammad Jiwa of Kedah in a retaliatory strike against the Bugis of Selangor, who had raided Kedah in 1770.[61] All they offered was a small defensive force to combat further assault, in return for which they were seeking the rights to all Kedah's port duties and much of its trade. This was obviously no bargain a Malay ruler could accept.[62] Batavia must have been cheered by this British ineptitude, and confided to the Directors its hope—somewhat optimistic, no doubt— that the failure of these missions would benefit Dutch trade, in particular the tin trade at Ujung Salang.[63] The urgency of the situation had been removed.

But in 1775, Governor Crans of Malacca wrote to Batavia of a new threat. The Raja of Selangor, estranged from his relations in Riau because of a feud with Daeng Kamboja, and fearing an attack by the combined forces of Kedah and Raja Ismail of Siak, had written to the English East India Company at Madras inviting them to establish a fortress in his territory.[64] There had been many precedents for such a step, from the offer of Singapore to the merchant Alexander Hamilton in 1710 to the invitation by Mansur Syah of Trengganu to the English to establish a post at his port in 1766.[65] The English Company had refused them all. But Crans himself was certain that in the new climate of trade, the English would accept the offer, to the great detriment of Malacca; for "the whole of the small trade of these Straits would be infringed, which would be most ruinous for Malacca, as this is at present the one thing which returns the greatest profit." And not only Malacca would be harmed; this was "a very serious matter that could greatly injure the Company;" if the English became established at Selangor, "great damage was to be expected not only to Malacca, but to Perak, which would rob the Company of the whole tin trade."[66]

Batavia, though never as concerned as Malacca with the tin trade, which it knew from long experience could not easily be controlled, nevertheless took the threat seriously enough to authorize Malacca to act against the Bugis in Selangor (without saying how), if reliable information were received that the English had acted on the offer.[67] They had not done so by the time Crans left Malacca in 1777, but he warned his successor, Governor de Bruijn, that "the intention of the Slangoor prince to give an establishment to these rivals of ours remains too evident from the favours of an unhindered trade which they enjoy, therefore Your Excellency should always keep one eye open in this direction, to crush that deed in the bud."[68]

It soon became plain that even without the benefit of an official post, the English, in cooperation with the Bugis, were rapidly capturing an increasing proportion of the trade of the Archipelago. After 1777, Malacca's tin collection declined; the only possible cause for this seems to have been the ever-increasing demand for the mineral by the English. By 1779, the amount of tin exported from the Straits by the English exceeded the whole amount delivered to the VOC.[69] Most of this tin sold to the English came from areas the VOC considered their exclusive preserve. For though Perak continued to deliver tin to Malacca, and the Sultan of Perak remained "the good friend" of Malacca, the ruler "appears not to have sufficient power over the lesser chiefs and *orang kaya* of his kingdom to prevent their smuggling trade with Slangoor."[70] Batavia was even more concerned about the large quantities of tin which were being shipped to the English via Riau from Bangka, a dependency of Palembang, which had now grown to be the VOC's major source of tin.[71]

Malaccan complaisance with the freedom with which the English utilized the Bugis ports during the early 1770s sprang from necessity, not choice, and Governor Crans was happy to note a growing rift in the Bugis leadership during the latter part of his term of office. Bugis-ruled Johor, unlike earlier versions of the polity, had two centers of power. Riau had to share power—and trade—with Selangor. As the phenomenal trade growth of the 1760s and 1770s increased the wealth of both, disagreement seems to have grown between the Selangor and the Riau Bugis. A traditional Malay ruler of Johor would have felt the need to subdue the rival port, and Daeng Kamboja cannot have been happy to see Selangor flourish; the Selangor Bugis themselves turned to Malay tradition, and enlisted the prestige of the Raja of Perak, scion of the oldest extant Malay ruling house (claiming descent from the old Malacca line) who installed the leader of the Selangor Bugis as Sultan of Selangor in 1766.[72] This further alienated Daeng Kamboja. In 1774, Malacca complained to the Riau regent about the "piratical" activities of Raja Ibrahim, son of the new Selangor Sultan, who had set himself up in the mouth of the Linggi River and was harassing trade there. Daeng Kamboja replied in strong terms, disassociating himself from Ibrahim's actions and requesting that the VOC dislodge him from the Linggi River, "for as long as he remains there he shall certainly ruin the traffic—although he is my relative I shall in no sense mix myself with such doings."[73] This vehemence may have been for Dutch ears, but the grievance with regard to being cut off from Linggi trade has a sincere ring; also, the establishment of the Sultanate in Selangor "without consulting me on the matter at all" seems to have rankled with Daeng Kamboja, who was now an old man. "Previously . . . no-one has ever become King in Selangor without the consent of the ruler of Johor, but now he is the first to have set himself up."[74] Daeng Kamboja also disapproved of the marriage of the Sultan of Selangor to a young member of the Perak royal household. As the prince Raja Haji, brother of the Selangor Raja, was deeply involved in all these events, he too was believed by the Dutch to be alienated from Daeng Kamboja. All these factors led the retiring Governor Jan Crans to advise his successor in

1777; "it is best to leave Riouw undisturbed for as long as the present prince Daeng Kamboja remains alive, for after his death, there will probably be great confusion, and if the Company then wished to help Malacca, I feel it would be easy to bring Riouw to submission."[75]

Events were to prove him wrong on both counts, but the advice to leave Riau "undisturbed" was wholly in keeping with a period in Dutch Malacca's history when, for once, fortune seemed to be smiling on the town, and continued peace was a worthwhile goal at which to aim. Even growing apprehensions concerning the English had been momentarily lulled by the failure of the English Company to gain a foothold in Aceh or Kedah, and the possibility that the detested Bugis might weaken themselves, as had so many Malay factions before them, in an internecine power struggle on the death of the strong Daeng Kamboja, made any thought of immediate intervention unnecessary. From 1759 to 1777 adherence to a strict neutrality in Malay affairs was no burden to the government of Malacca, as the prosperity which came to the Straits with the growing country trade spilled over into Malacca's treasury and relieved it, for a time, of the dilemma of having to keep Malacca both poor enough, and rich enough, to satisfy its masters in Batavia.

NOTES

1. Kol. Arch. 2827, Malacca to Batavia (6 February 1758): 18.

2. Kol. Arch. 3387, Governor Crans' Report on Malacca (1777): 538.

3. Ibid.

4. Harrison, "Malacca in the 18th century," 31.

5. See Appendix II.

6. Netscher, *Djohor*, 106. In 1774 we find him writing to Malacca to express his thanks "to the Malacca people for their help to his children." Kol. Arch. 3335, Daeng Kamboja to Malacca (27 March 1774); cited in Malacca to Batavia (31 January 1775): 9.

7. SSR, 1, Light to Andrew Ross, (1 February 1769): 144.

8. L. Andaya, *Kingdom of Johor*, 280.

9. van der Chijs, *Plakaatboek*, 7: 257–61.

10. Kol. Arch. 2776, Malacca to Batavia (4 February 1757): 12.

11. Kol. Arch. 2858, Malacca to Batavia (19 October 1759): 15–16.

12. Kol. Arch. 2863, Generale Missiven (31 December 1760): 549.

13. Batavia to Malacca (25 June 1761): 260.

14. Netscher, *Djohor*, 38–39.

15. Ibid. 130–33.

16. Kol. Arch. 3020, Generale Missiven (31 December 1765): 1587.

17. Batavia to Malacca (15 October 1765): 157.

18. Kol. Arch. 3387, Governor Crans' Memorie (1777): 544.

19. Kol. Arch. 3391, Malacca to Batavia [Secret] (10 February 1777): 92–94.

20. Kol. Arch. 3362, Malacca to Batavia [Secret] (15 January 1776): 341.

21. Kol. Arch. 3387, Governor Crans' Memorie (1777): 543.

22. Kol. Arch. 2857, Malacca to Batavia (6 February 1758): 19.

23. Kol. Arch. 2858, Mansur Syah to Malacca, Malacca to Batavia (11 December 1759): 30.

24. According to the *Tuhfat,* the court was about to set out for Trengganu when a quarrel broke out between Mansur Syah and Sultan Sulaiman's son, the Raja di Baruh. Mansur hurried his departure to escape. "So no Riau people went to Trengganu, except for those boats already at sea, which Raja Kecik (Mansur Syah) took to Trengganu with many princes. On that day there was great confusion in Riau, as though it were the assembly for the Day of Judgement, because some had been separated from their parents, and some from their brothers and sisters, and because those who had already gone aboard the boats of their parents and families had left their husbands and brothers ashore." Raja Ali Haji ibn Ahmad, *The Precious Gift,* 109–10.

25. Kol. Arch. 2858, Malacca to Batavia (10 March 1759): 72. In this demographically underdeveloped area the loss of population was a fundamental problem to a ruler.

26. Raja Ali Haji ibn Ahmad, *The Precious Gift,* 113.

27. Kol. Arch. 2891, Generale Missiven (31 December 1761): 680.

28. Kol. Arch. 2916, Malacca to Batavia (6 March 1761): 8–9.

29. Raja Ali Haji ibn Ahmad, *The Precious Gift,* 122–24.

30. Ibid. 127–33.

31. Ibid. 137.

32. Kol. Arch. 2891, Generale Missiven (31 December 1761): 680.

33. Kol. Arch. 2921, Generale Missiven (18 October 1762): 27. van der Chijs, *Realia* 2: 185.

34. van der Chijs, Plakaatboek 8: 853.

35. Ibid. 858–59.

36. Ibid. 902.

37. Kol. Arch. 2858, Malacca to Batavia (10 March 1759): 79.

38. Kol. Arch. 2893, Generale Missiven (31 December 1760): 352.

39. Kol. Arch. 3045, Malacca to Batavia (14 September 1765): 25, 16–18.

40. Ibid. 23.

41. Kol. Arch. 3387, Governor Crans' Memorie (1777): 538.

42. H. D. Dodwell, A Calendar of Madras Dispatches 1745–1765, 1: 261

43. Lewis, "Kedah," 36–43.

44. Kol. Arch. 2753, Captain Gerrit Zeeman's Report (19 June 1755): 25.

45. Elephants were Perak's second most important export. Kol. Arch. 3045, Malacca to Batavia (25 January 1765): 19.

46. Kol. Arch. 2891, Generale Missiven (31 December 1761): 685.

47. John Dunmore, "French Visitors to Trengganu in the 18th Century," *JMBRAS,* 45.1 (1973): 145–60.

48. Kol. Arch. 2783, Generale Missiven (31 December 1757): 646.

49. Kol. Arch. 2776, Malacca to Batavia (9 April 1756): 33.

50. Batavia to Malacca (14 September 1762): 520.

51. The Malaccan Shipping Lists (Boomboeken) do not mention any Chinese junks for the first half of the century, though Indian shipping is noted. But in 1761 thirty, and in 1764 thirty-seven, Chinese vessels arrived at Malacca. Kol. Arch. 2954, Malacca Boomboeken (1761), Aangekomende, and Kol. Arch. 3045, Malacca's Boomboeken (1764), Aangekomende.

52. Plakaatboek 8, (13 May 1765): 28.

53. Kol. Arch. 3052, Generale Missiven (31 December 1766): 873.

54. van der Chijs, *Plakaatboek,* 8: 841.

55. Ibid. 10: 227.

56. Kol. Arch. 3446, Malacca to Batavia (12 February 1779): 122–26.

57. B. Andaya, *Perak,* 244–45.

58. Bassett, "British Trade and Policy," *B.K.I.* (1964): 197.

59. Bassett, "British Commercial and Strategic Interests," 126–30.

60. Kol. Arch. 3144, Generale Missiven (31 December 1769): 811.

61. Lewis, "Kedah," 40. And see B. Andaya, *Perak,* 293–306.

62. Bassett, "British Commercial and Strategic Interests," 128.

63. Batavia to Malacca (31 May 1773): 11.

64. Kol. Arch. 3362, Malacca to Batavia (6 March 1775): 333.

65. Kol. Arch. 3052, Generale Missiven (31 December 1766): 872. Daeng Kamboja had also "proposed to have an English resident to reside on Pulo Bijang (an island near Riau)," in1769. The Dutch may not have been aware of this offer made to Light in 1769. SSR 1: 144.

66. Kol. Arch. 3387, Governor Crans' Memorie (1777): 539 and 541. See also Kol. Arch. 3362, Malacca to Batavia [Secret] (6 March 1775).

67. Kol. Arch. 3387, Governor Crans' Memorie (1777): 540.

68. Ibid. 541.

69. Kol. Arch. 3446, Malacca to Batavia (12 Feb 1779): 53.

70. Ibid. 51.

71. Ibid. 53.

72. See B. Andaya, "The Installation of the First Sultan of Selangor in 1766," *JMBRAS,* 47.1 (1974): 41–57.

73. Kol. Arch. 3335, Daeng Kamboja to the Governor of Malacca, (27 March 1774).

74. Ibid.

75. Kol. Arch. 3387, Governor Crans' Memorie (1777): 538.

6

NEUTRALITY ABANDONED— THE DUTCH CAPTURE OF RIAU

IN 1777 Daeng Kamboja died at Riau. His son Raja Ali informed the VOC at Batavia of his death. Governor Crans of Malacca had predicted that turmoil would break out between the different Bugis factions on the death of Daeng Kamboja, and, acting on this prediction and the assumption that the new Bugis ruler of Riau would be in a weakened position, Batavia responded with a letter protesting the frequent breaking of the 1758 treaty between Johor and the VOC, especially those articles that required the ruler of Riau to exclude "foreign Europeans" and merchants without VOC passes from the port.[1]

However, it rapidly became clear that Crans had misjudged events, and the major rift in the Bugis ranks that he had predicted was not going to occur. Raja Ali was unable to make good his claim to succeed his father, and the office passed instead, in the customary fashion, to his cousin, Raja Haji, son of the second Bugis Raja Muda, Daeng Cellak, a brother and strong ally of the first Sultan of Selangor. Raja Haji was at Pontianak in Kalimantan when he was informed of his uncle's death, and he sailed for Riau, but altered course for Pahang as he neared the Riau coast. In Pahang he secured the support of the Bendahara of Johor who installed him as Raja Muda.[2] Sultan Mahmud and another son of Daeng Kamboja, Raja Abd al-Samad, sailed to meet him in Pahang, and he took up the rule of Riau without further opposition. The rift was healed, and the Bugis were strengthened and brought together under the rule of this charismatic warrior.

Raja Haji had gained a formidable reputation as a religious zealot (as his name implies, he had made the pilgrimage to Mecca) and fighting leader in the constant small wars of Kalimantan and the Straits, not qualities likely to make him a submissive opponent. Good relations with Selangor were restored, and the port of Riau became busier than ever. "There were several happy years because [Riau] was at peace and prosperous, famed for its cheap food and for the amount of profit traders could make there."³ Malacca's Governor de Bruijn was quick to complain that the new Raja Muda "threw open the trade there to all and sundry without the slightest attention to our protests and warnings about the violation of existing treaties between the VOC and Johoor."⁴

Faced with a strong Bugis ruler where they had thought to find a weakened one, and with ever-increasing Bugis depredations (to feed the constantly growing trade with the English) on areas that it regarded as its own sphere of influence in the Straits, Batavia was at last driven to make some positive effort to curb Riau's trade. Characteristically, Batavia's first move struck at Malacca as well as Riau. In 1778, the central government prohibited the traffic of Chinese junks to any port in the Straits, or indeed to anywhere in the Archipelago, except Batavia. Batavia had attempted to restrict this trade before, but without success. This new order was very restrictive; no junks were to go to "Malacca, Johor or Riouw [Riau], Atjeh [Aceh], Passir or elsewhere in those seas," and provision was made for the strict enforcement of this rule. Anyone who defied the new rule was to have his vessel confiscated. Notice of this trade restriction was posted in Dutch and Chinese at Malacca and Batavia, and communicated to Chinese merchants at Canton by the VOC's supercargos there. Nachodas leaving the roads in China were given written notice in Chinese, and copies of the order were also sent to Amoy.⁵

This measure drew an immediate response from Raja Haji, but it was not couched in the submissive or conciliatory vein that the Dutch would doubtless have liked. In March, 1779 Malacca received a letter from Raja Haji requesting that the Chinese trade at Riau be allowed to continue. The letter voiced complaints of the way he and his subjects had been treated by the VOC. The new Raja Muda of Riau claimed that

Malacca had "acted against the old friendship" which had long existed between the VOC and Johor by claiming that vessels coming to the Dutch port but not disembarking cargo there still had to pay toll and submit to being searched. Even vessels owned by members of the Sultan's family now had to pay toll. This was not merely an economic grievance for the Johorese—it was a grave breach of manners on the part of the Malaccan Dutch to treat the *anak raja* as ordinary beings, and if Raja Haji had seen fit to mention it, he obviously was not in the mood to make any concessions to the Dutch. Raja Haji also argued that the VOC could have no complaints about the sale of such prohibited goods as spices at Riau, as these goods had all been obtained from the Company's own stocks, (no doubt through the connivance of corrupt VOC employees). No attempt was made to answer the other Dutch accusations, and no reference was made to the VOC's desire to renew the old treaty of alliance between Johor and the VOC.[6]

After consulting Batavia, Malacca replied to Raja Haji's letter in detail, and without backing away from the issues. The general restrictions on Chinese trade could not be relaxed, at least not until Raja Haji showed himself willing to fulfill his commitments to the VOC. It was freely admitted that some vessels en route from Riau to Selangor, which stopped in but did not unload cargo at Malacca, were charged toll. This was done "because of the breaking of the treaty [of 1758] by Johor, and the great harm being done to this place [Malacca] by supplying Slangoor directly with goods formerly bought here."[7] Malacca denied that royal vessels had ever been taxed.[8] Toll-free trade for the Johor *orang kaya* had always been a sore point in Malacca; in the view of the Company administrators, the Johorese tended to abuse this privilege consistently.[9] Now that Malacca depended so heavily on its tolls for income, the admission of the numerous dependents of the Riau *orang kaya* toll-free was likely to be particularly abhorrent to the authorities. The Malacca government argued that they had no way of ascertaining whether vessels which produced the Raja Muda's *chiap* had the right to do so.

But Malacca laid most stress on the continued foreign European trade to Riau, which was admitted contrary to the stipulations of the 1758 treaty with Johor, and in this they had the full support of Batavia. They argued that the Company had never granted any passes allowing European ships to call at Riau, and that these ships should not be admitted to the southern port. Any vessel that came without a VOC pass, or brought goods not listed on that pass, would be treated as a smuggling craft. Raja Haji was warned once more that if he wished the Company to regard him as their friend, he must confiscate and declare all items, especially tin and pepper, brought into Riau without a pass from the VOC.[10] This almost certainly reflects growing Dutch unease at the continuing collaboration of the Bugis and the English country traders, and an underlying fear that it might grow into a more formal alliance.

European politics were responsible for some of this unease. Relations between England and the Netherlands had deteriorated in Europe and Asia, as the Netherlands had been drawn into the French sphere of influence in the continuing conflict between England and France. In view of this, the English Company seemed unlikely to give up the idea of an outpost in the Straits, and the Dutch must have seen, as the English were beginning to, that Riau was ideally situated to become such a post.[11]

Raja Haji, though continuing to protest his total lack of desire, or capacity, to damage the Dutch Company (he was to the VOC, he declared, "as a man of eighty was to a young prince")[12] was not prepared to go to great lengths to mollify the Company. He answered none of Malacca's charges; he did not even send the customary gift with his reply, or return proper thanks for the Company's gift. He concluded his letter with a request that the Dutch send him five iron cannons.[13] Not surprisingly, the request was denied.

This exchange closed the correspondence between Malacca and Raja Haji for a time. Malacca now proceeded to take every step possible, short of open warfare, to curtail the "smuggling" trade of the Bugis. Cruisers were sent to patrol the Linggi River, north of Malacca, and the Larut River in Perak.[14] Again this was not merely a Malaccan initiative—Batavia seemed just as firmly opposed to the continued growth of Riau's trade. The Governor-General initiated investigations in Palembang to uncover the principal tin-smugglers there, in the hope of cutting off Riau from a major source of tin. By 1782 Dutch officials at Palembang had drawn up a list of nineteen Palembangers and twelve people from Riau involved in the trade; Batavia "hoped that now the King [of Palembang], with this specific information, will have more success in suppressing the smuggling."[15]

Meanwhile, relations with England in Europe continued to deterio-rate, even as English trade through the Straits grew. In June, 1780 news arrived in Malacca from India that England had declared war on the Netherlands the previous December. English sea-power in the Bay of Bengal was weak compared to that of the Dutch ally, France; there was no immediate threat to Batavia, but Malacca was more vulnerable. Malacca petitioned for more European troops to strengthen their forces, for they were uncertain as to how far they could trust the Asians who formed the bulk of their manpower.[16]

For the moment, Malacca appeared to be in more danger from the Bugis than the English. Raja Haji may have been encouraged by the news of Anglo-Dutch hostilities to move against the Company; or he may have felt that, as in the 1757–58 conflict (in which he himself had played no small part), the best defense against growing Dutch-Malay cooperation was attack. In 1781 Malacca was informed by Batavia that Raja Haji and his nephew, Ibrahim of Selangor, had sent envoys to the ruler of Bone in Sulawesi, "not only to express continued friendship but offering to come to his assistance in times of need."[17] The Malaccan gov-ernment immediately suspected that this projected alliance was aimed at them. Governor de Bruijn wrote to the Bugis leaders, informing them that he was aware of their mission to Bone, and that Malacca was prepared for any hostile moves they could make. Bone needed no other ally than the VOC, he declared, and all thought of future correspon-dence with Bone must be abandoned if these princes did not wish to arouse the suspicion that they had tried to win Bone away from the bonds of the Company. "For," he concluded, "I fear that the Company otherwise will employ force to prevent this possibility, which will be dis-agreeable to my friend."[18] A rumor that a fleet of ships was being fitted out at Selangor and Riau, relayed by the head of the Malaccan garrison in Perak, further aroused de Bruijn's suspicions. The rumor proved false, but the suspicions remained.[19]

Raja Haji may have been alarmed at the hostility he had stirred up at Malacca, for he now became more conciliatory. He assured de Bruijn that his communications with Bone were innocent in intent, and that he harbored no ill designs against the Malaccan Government.[20] In May, 1782, he sent a mission to Batavia, officially, (and belatedly) notifying the VOC of his accession to the post of Raja Muda (and confusing them in the process), and expressing his desire to maintain Johor's alliance with the VOC. The letters were accompanied by the normal request that his envoys be granted toll-free trade at Batavia.[21] The Governor-General, acting in the apparent misapprehension that the original Raja Haji had died and this mission came from a friendlier source,[22] received the Riau party more heartily than might otherwise have been the case. An official letter to the "new" Raja Muda of Riau in June, 1782, wished him well in his new high office, and urged him to send a mission to Malacca to renew the old friendship between the Company and Johor.[23] Malacca too sent a letter and accompanying gift to Riau in August, once again urging Raja Haji to send an envoy to Malacca empowered to renew the VOC's contract with Johor—and especially, in this instance, to discuss the matter of the division of spoils from prize-ships which Raja Haji was helping the Malacca forces to capture.[24] Raja Haji duly promised to do so, though de Bruijn seriously doubted that the Riau ruler was sincere in this, or would ever be willing to bind himself to the Company, or put a stop to the trade of Riau, especially in tin and pepper.

In October, 1782, a major confrontation between Malacca and the Bugis developed. Raja Haji himself came with a large force to Muar, just south of Malacca. He sent two emissaries to the Dutch fortress, "not only to inform us of his arrival at this place, but that he came here intending to go to Malacca because he had no fit messengers to send to discuss the matters raised by Commissioner Rappa" during his recent visit to Riau. Abrahim de Wind was then sent to Muar to discover whether the prince wished to come to Malacca to draw up a new treaty and sign a convention against the English.[25]

De Wind's subsequent report ended any hopes the Dutch may have harbored about Raja Haji's intentions to co-operate with the VOC. After initially experiencing difficulty in gaining an audience with the Bugis leader, de Wind found Raja Haji unconciliatory, answering his questions about a new treaty in an arrogant "and more or less ruffled" manner.[26] The Raja Muda asserted that there already existed a contract between Johor and the Dutch Company to which he had always held true; that he had no power to forbid the trade in pepper and tin in the kingdom of Johor "for his subjects were of old accustomed to carry on a free trade"; that the prohibited items in any case originated in the territory of the Company itself, and if the Dutch wished to prevent them being exported they had the means to do so; the Dutch and the English Companies were great powers, next to whom he was practically helpless, and he could not therefore take part in any struggle between them; and, finally, that an English ship had been overpowered and carried off from within his jurisdiction.[27]

This final point centered on the capture of the English ship *Betsy* in Riau by a French privateer in February, 1782, and highlights Raja Haji's difficult position in the continuing Anglo-Dutch War, as a formal (though unenthusiastic) ally of the Dutch, but still heavily dependent on English trade for the prosperity of himself and his subjects. The matter presents a fascinating detail in the larger picture of Raja Haji's relations with both the Dutch and the English at this time. Malay sources tend to be uninformative on such small-scale and immediate matters, and in any case, Raja Haji was reputed to be "very secretive in his plans," and would reveal them to no-one before they ripened.[28] The reference, in Malacca's letter of August, 1782, to Raja Haji, to division of spoils from prize-ships Raja Haji helped Malacca to capture, indicates some agreement between the Dutch and the Bugis prince—though this would seem to have gone quite against the interests of Riau's trade. Was this a Dutch attempt to place a wedge between the English and the Bugis? Had Raja Haji, or his servants, been tempted by the thought of easy pickings? Or was the *Betsy* a victim of the ongoing intrigue between the Bugis and Malay groups? The Dutch records do not supply an answer to this riddle; the Bugis narrative, the *Tuhfat al-Nafis* indicates that Raja Haji had indeed entered into some arrangement with the Dutch, but gives no details. But the capture of the *Betsy* was undoubtedly the cause of his openly seeking a quarrel with Malacca at this juncture, despite his relatively recent attempts at peace. Perhaps the warrior in his nature overrode counsels of discretion when faced with this challenge. Be that as it may, with his force of 2600 men which "daily increased," Raja Haji was far too close to Malacca for the VOC's comfort.

The Malacca government, now thoroughly alarmed by the force congregating at Muar, feared to receive the Bugis at Malacca. They considered the mission a possible ruse to gain entry to the Dutch fortress, and decided not to send further European envoys to see Raja Haji in case they were held as hostages. Instead, the Regent of Rokan, who had recently come to Malacca to speak for Siak, was sent to Muar to tell Raja

Haji that if he wanted to deal further with the Company he must send letters or representatives to Malacca. Governor de Bruijn felt that it had become necessary to show Raja Haji his suspicions clearly, so that the latter "would not pursue a plan to come to Malacca in a friendly guise, and so attack the town."[29] Meanwhile an urgent plea was sent to Batavia for reinforcements, in case the Bugis decided on an open attack.

The Regent of Rokan reported to the Dutch that Raja Haji had come to Muar to gain compensation for the capture of the English ship *Betsy*; he demanded a quarter of the prize money for the captured ship, and if the Company would not consent to these terms, he would become their open and declared enemy. This action had, the Bugis leader claimed, been forced on him by the resentment of the English, and the bitter reproaches which were piled on him daily by his subjects, both the nobles and common people alike, many of whom depended on the English trade for their livelihood. In September, 1782, five English ships had by-passed Riau to punish him for his part in the capture of the *Betsy*.[30]

The Malacca government felt the need to act firmly against this attempted intimidation. They wrote to Batavia that, faced with this ulti-matum, they had decided not to pay even the small douceur that had been authorized for Raja Haji's part in the capture of the *Betsy*. Instead they informed him that Johor's contract with the VOC forbade the admission of foreign ships without an official pass, and therefore the *Betsy*'s presence in Riau had been, in any case, illegal. They added that he had not at the time made any attempt to assert the neutrality of his port, and that his demand for a quarter of the prize money was unrea-sonable.[31] Raja Haji left Muar on the 17th of October to return to Riau, where Governor de Bruijn believed he intended to raise a stronger force. His departure coincided with news from India that an English fleet, rumored to be headed for Malacca, was embarking many men.

The Dutch at Malacca and Batavia now decided that forceful action must be taken to bring the Bugis threat to an end before they could openly join with the English, who had already occupied the Dutch out-post at Perak in 1781.[32] The Governor-General wrote in November, 1782, that "the humiliation of [Raja Haji] is now a necessity, as much to punish him for his unjust aggressions as to warn the neighboring princes against following his example."[33] There still appeared to be no immediate danger from the English, who "will not at present be able to give the Bugis any worthwhile assistance," presumably because of their naval weakness to the east of the Bay of Bengal, which stemmed from the lack of a safe port in the area. A small fleet was sent immediately from Malacca to blockade Riau; in the expectation of reinforcements from Batavia, Trengganu or Siak, no attempt was to be made to attack the port until these new forces arrived. Batavia sent the warships *'t Hoff ter Linde* and *Dolphin,* but Malacca's Malay allies were less prompt.[34]

The Malay princes still looked to Malacca for an alternative to the growing power of Raja Haji. Rembau had concluded a new agreement with the VOC,[35] and requested that Dutch cruisers be sent to patrol the Linggi River to keep the Bugis out.[36] Other guardships were sent to the Larut River in Perak where the Bugis "appear to have lost their credit with the king and a number of the *orang kaya,* though unfortunately some of the latter "still made common cause with [them]."[37] Trengganu also remained the firm enemy of the Bugis. But none of these princes were at this time in a position to assist the Dutch in a war with the Bugis; Mansur Syah, the most determined opponent of the Bugis, was fully occupied in waging a war with his northern neighbor Kelantan.

The blockade of Riau was maintained for the better part of a year, disrupting trade there, so that, as the *Tuhfat* tells us, "Rice and other foodstuffs became expensive, while trading *perahu* attempting to enter ran the risk of seizure by the warships which tried to intercept them. Some got through, others did not."[38] An English observer, Captain Francis Light, wrote: "They [the Dutch] stationed some of their vessels in the tract through which the Bugis vessels from Borneo and Celebes always come, and under decoy of English colours, they seized numbers of vessels that came that way, plundered them, and put the crews to death, without sparing a man ... the blockade continued for six months, during which no vessel of any nation was allowed to approach the place."[39]

But the Dutch did not account their success to be as great as Light reported; finally Batavia was moved to send reinforcements, and "ordered that two delegates of our [Malaccan] Council should have command of the expedition. Vice-Governor Lemker and Syahbandar Hoynck van Papendrecht were given this task."[40] When the reinforcements joined the blockading fleet, it was at last decided to attempt an attack on Riau. This proved to be a costly mistake, for in the treacherous waters off Riau the Dutch were at a disadvantage. Their three largest vessels ran aground, and the flagship was blown up with the Commander of the expedition, Vice-Governor Arnold Francis Lemker, aboard. A Dutch eye witness, Hoynck van Papendrecht, wrote to his family: "The wreck remained burning for three days in the channel through which we had to pass. In the meantime the spring tide had subdued, and the blowing up of the *Melax Welvaart* had deprived us of the flower of our crews and of our strongest vessel. The council of war took the unanimous decision to raise the siege, we being in want of everything and far too inferior in strength."[41]

Malacca's attempt to coerce Raja Haji had failed ignominiously, even with the help of Batavia. The fleet arrived back at Malacca on the 24 January 1784 to find the town already under counterattack by a force of Selangor Bugis.[42]

On 14 January 1784 Raja Ibrahim of Selangor had landed at Batang Tiga, just north of Malacca. Skirmishing broke out immediately, but the Bugis established a foothold on shore. On the 16 January "it was reported that the enemy were actively occupied in preparing stockades at Batang Tiga, and in burning houses at Batang Tiga and at Tanjung Keling. Firing continued there the whole day, and the following night."[43] When the siege of Riau was raised, the Bugis did not depart, but sent to Raja Haji to join them at Malacca. This caused some debate at Riau. The Riau Bugis were not wholeheartedly in support of a new attack on Malacca, even after the Dutch blockade.

> However, at that time there were many differences of opinion among the Riau princes; some of them approved of Yang Dipertuan Muda Raja Haji's going to Malacca, and some, like Raja Ali and Raja Abd al-Samad, sons of the late Bearded One [Daeng Kamboja] did not. This led to misunderstandings amongst them.
> According to the story Yang Dipertuan Muda Raja Haji was intent on going . . .[44]

Raja Haji enforced his will, and the Riau Bugis joined the siege on the 13 February 1784, landing at Teluk Ketapang to the south of Malacca. There followed months of skirmishing. Malacca was surrounded on the landward side but there was still access from the sea—on May 5 a sampan arrived from Siak, "having on board Abd al-Bahir, envoy of the old King of Siak, Raja Muhammad Ali" who sent a letter to de Bruijn, and "the Malay Abdul Moehit," who had been sent on a commission to Trengganu in 1783 and had returned via Siak. Malacca's fleet had therefore kept the sea-ways open, though it could not drive off the Bugis. On May 14 Raja Muhammad Ali came from Siak in person. But the siege, which continued six months, laid a great strain on Malacca's garrison, which was no longer kept at full strength.[45]

Despite this continued communication with Siak and Trengganu, no Malay allies had come to their aid by May. Englishman Francis Light believed that "the fate of the town is doubtful,"[46] and the Malaccan Syahbandar van Papendrecht wrote retrospectively of this period:

> We were in great embarrassment. Pieter de Bruijn, inexperienced and timorous, shut himself up in the fort, the new Vice Governor, a valorous and capable gentleman, took the command in the outlying works on one side and I took charge on the other side. The enemy hemmed us in so closely, except on the sea-side.[47]

But Raja Haji's success was to be short lived. Relief for Malacca was at hand, though from an unexpected quarter. "Admiral van Braam came with the Government squadron to relieve us, in which he would not have succeeded but for the death of Radja Hadji, in whom all the natives saw . . . [a living saint]."[48]

The government fleet which came so fortuitously to Malacca's aid was a Netherlands State (not VOC) force of six capital ships and six smaller vessels, sent to Asia in an attempt to shore up the waning power of the VOC. The Dutch had faired very badly in the Fourth Anglo-Dutch War, though not in the Straits of Malacca, where they had been protected by the French fleet. The loss of Perak in December, 1781, was the worst blow Malacca had suffered. The Netherlands fleet arrived at Malacca on the 29 May 1784; it could not have come at a better time. Even in the face of this powerful new force, as van Papendrecht indicates, the Bugis did not call off the attack. It was not until the 18th of June, when Raja Haji was killed in battle, that the Bugis siege of Malacca was finally broken.[49]

After the death of Raja Haji, the attack on Malacca virtually crumbled away. On 13 July Admiral Jacob van Braam, the commander of the Netherlands government fleet, followed the retreating Bugis to Selangor, where with the aid of fourteen vessels sent by Malacca's somewhat belated ally, Muhammad Ali of Siak, they forced Sultan Ibrahim and his supporters to flee inland to Pahang. Van Braam installed Muhammad Ali as ruler of Selangor, where he was to be represented by his nephew Sayid Ali.[50] Van Braam then turned his attention to Riau, which two Malacca vessels had been blockading since the beginning of August.

When the news of Raja Haji's death reached Riau, Daeng Kamboja's son, Raja Ali, had been appointed Raja Muda. The new Raja Muda, ironically that same Raji Ali previously welcomed to the post by Batavia, first tried conciliation, and when that failed attempted to fortify the port.[51] But van Braam's fleet was greatly superior to the Malaccan force that Raja Haji had humiliated the previous year, and on the 29th of October, 1784, the Bugis were defeated in a fiercely contested battle off Riau. Raja Ali fled with "those of Bugis descent, whoever could avail themselves of the opportunity." The mass withdrawal of the Bugis followers of Raja Ali meant that the young Sultan Mahmud was left alone with his Malay advisers to face the Dutch Admiral.

The resulting treaty ended Johor's independence.[52] Never again was a Bugis to be appointed to the office of raja muda or to any other high office in Johor. The Sultan was to make no decision without consulting his four Malay ministers. No European shipping was to be admitted to the ports of Johor and Pahang. Asian traders were allowed to enter the port, but not those from Sulawesi or Kalimantan, nor any bringing spices or tin from Palembang. The VOC could confiscate any tin brought from Palembang in defiance of this order for 15 rds per bahar. Tin imported to Riau from places other than Palembang was to be delivered to the VOC for a fixed price of 36 rds per bahar. A Dutch garrison was established at Tanjung Pinang, in the harbor of Riau. A complement of 254 men was left to man this stronghold when van Braam left Riau at the end of November; the captain of this force was warned to be on guard as much against attempts by the English to retake the port as by the Bugis. The first Resident was installed in Riau on 19 June 1785.[53] The Batavian government was determined that Riau would never again act, as it had from 1761 to 1784, as a center for the English country trade in the Archipelago.

1. Batavia to Malacca (28 April 1778) and Batavia to Malacca (11 June 1778): 309.

2. Raja Ali Haji ibn Ahmad, *The Precious Gift,* 159.

3. Ibid. 161.

4. Cited in Harrison, "Trade in the Straits of Malacca in 1785," 56.

5. Kol. Arch. 3396, Biljet by the High Goverment (1 May 1778).

6. Kol. Arch. 3474, Raja Haji to Malacca (March 1779).

7. Ibid. Malacca to Raja Haji (20 December 1779).

8. It should be noted that Batavia had passed a resolution in May 1779 prohibiting this very practice. Van der Chijs, *Realia* 2: 188 (11 May 1779).

9. A dispute about this privilege had occurred in the reign of the last Malay Raja Muda; see chapter 2.

10. Kol. Arch. 3474, Malacca to Raja Haji, (20 December 1779).

11. See Nicholas Tarling, *Anglo-Dutch Rivalry in the Malay World 1780–1824.* English scouts finally started to recommend Riau as the future British commercial center in the archipelago about 1783. Bassett, "British Commercial and Strategic Interests," 130.

12. Kol. Arch. 3474, Malacca to Batavia (20 December 1779).

13. Ibid.

14. Kol. Arch. 3474, Malacca to Batavia (14 February 1780): 34–36.

15. Kol. Arch. 3499, Generale Missiven (31 December 1782): 1171.

16. Kol. Arch. 3485, Malacca to Batavia [Secret] (17 August 1781): 2414–20.

17. Kol. Arch. 3495, Malacca to Raja Haji (1781).

18. Ibid.

19. Kol. Arch. 3495, Malacca to Batavia [Secret] (7 December 1781): 183.

20. Ibid. 184.

21. van der Chijs, *Realia* 2: 188.

22. Kol. Arch. 3499, Generale Missiven (31 December 1782): 1182. "The Regent of Riau Raja Haji is dead, and has been succeeded under the same name by his son-in-law, who has advised us of this succession by a considerable embassy."

23. Netscher, Djohor, 170.

24. Kol. Arch. 3499, Malacca to Batavia (14 October 1782): 892.

25. Ibid. 893.

26. Kol. Arch. 3499, Abraham de Wind, Report on his Mission to Muar (9 October 1782): 902–03.

27. Ibid. 905.

28. Kol. Arch. 3499, Malacca to Batavia, Secret (14 October 1782): 895.

29. Ibid. 897–98.

30. Kol. Arch. 3499, Malacca to Batavia (15 October 1782): 908–09.

31. Ibid. 909–10.

32. B. Andaya, Perak, 344–46.

33. Batavia to Malacca (17 November 1782).

34. Kol. Arch. 3499, Instructions to Captains Toger Abo and Christian F. Winter Heim, of the ships *Dolphin* and *'t Hoff ter Linde*, (17 November 1782): 931.

35. Heeres and Stapel, *Corpus Diplomaticum*, 6: 424–28.

36. Kol. Arch. 3474, Malacca to Batavia (14 February 1780): 34.

37. Ibid. 34–66.

38. Raja Ali Haji ibn Ahmad, *The Precious Gift*, 168.

39. SSR vol. 1, Light to Andrew Ross (1784): 150.

40. P. C. Hoynk van Papendrecht, "Some Old Private Letters from the Cape, Batavia and Malacca, (1778–1888)," *JMBRAS* 2.1 (1924): 21.

41. Ibid. 21–22. [Note- The *Daghregister* calls it a "Small vessel"]

42. W. E. Maxwell, "Raja Haji," JSBRAS 22 (1890): 190–91.

43. Ibid. 189.

44. Raja Ali Haji ibn Ahmad, *The Precious Gift*, 171–72.

45. Sonnerat, *Voyages*, 20.

46. SSR vol. 1, Light to Andrew Ross (1784): 150.

47. van Papendrecht, "Some Old Letters," 22. (van Papendrecht had earlier written contemptuously of the Governor as "a Ceylonese who knows only secretarial work . . . By his bad correspondence, mistaken reports, etc, he led into error and exposed all our fleets." Ibid. 22

48. Ibid 23

49. Maxwell, "Raja Haji," 205.

50. Netscher, *Djohor*, 138.

51. Ibid. 190. Netscher notes a letter sent from Raja Ali to the Governor of Malacca, and a reply to the same, the contents of which are lost. After the reply arrived, however, Raja Ali proceeded to fortify Riau.

52. *Surat-Surat perdjandjian antara Kesultan Riau dengan pemerintahan*², 3–31.

53. Netscher, *Djohor*, 204.

7

THE VOC'S "FORWARD
MOVEMENT" IN THE
STRAITS OF MALACCA

In 1784 Batavia was not content, as it had been in 1759, to relieve Malacca and then withdraw from the Straits. The Dutch swiftly followed up their victory at Malacca with successful operations in Selangor and Riau, forcing the rulers of both places not merely to grant the usual commercial concessions, but to acknowledge the VOC as their territorial overlord. Moreover, they left garrisons to ensure that the treaties would be enforced. They claimed the territories of Johor and Pahang by right of conquest. As Siak had been ceded to them by Sultan Sulaiman in 1746, this made the VOC now the largest territorial power in the Malacca Straits, with a claim to all the old territories of the Johor Empire on either side of the Straits.

Raja Ali and his followers sought refuge in Mempawah (in Kalimantan), with a son of Daeng Menambun, brother of Raja Ali's grandfather Daeng Parani, and tried to redeem the situation in the traditional way, (as even the Dutch in Malacca expected him to) by establishing a new entrepôt to continue his father's lucrative trade with the English. Leaving Mempawah for the neighboring Sukadana, where with his Bugis following and some Illanuns from the Sulu Archipelago he attempted to set up a new headquarters. Almost his first move was to write urgently to the English, who had been on the point of setting up an official station in Riau just before the Dutch conquest.[1]

But he was not left in peace long enough to receive an answer to his appeal. The VOC made use of an alliance with the ambitious ruler of Pontianak to drive the Bugis from this new potential port early in 1786. Raja Ali retreated to Siantan, which, however, does not appear to have been a suitable site for a major entrepôt. The VOC and the Pontianak ruler went on to blockade Mempawah. The arrival of the second Netherlands State naval squadron in June, 1787 enabled them to press home the attack successfully and add Mempawah to the growing list of their subject territories.[2]

Things had not been going quite so smoothly for the VOC in Selangor, where the Dutch had left Sayid Ali of Siak in control. A number of Selangor chiefs disavowed the new regime, and at their request the VOC began to rule Selangor directly in mid-1785.[3] In June of that year the Sultan of Selangor, Ibrahim, Raja Haji's nephew, returned from Pahang and with the help of the Johor Bendahara (now established in Pahang), succeeded in driving out the Dutch garrison. He too sent an immediate plea to the English East India Company for help.[4] But the Dutch blockaded the Selangor River closely and, deprived of access to the country trade and the means of importing provisions,[5] Ibrahim was forced to capitulate to the VOC in June, 1786, before he had received any answer from the English or heard of their projected settlement at Penang. Worn down by the Dutch blockade, on 29 July 1786 he signed a treaty acknowledging that Selangor belonged to the VOC by right of conquest. Ibrahim was to remain ruler, but trade, especially the tin trade—his main source of revenue—was to be carried on in future only with the Dutch Company. The results of this monopoly, which the VOC enforced with patrol ships, was that by 1789 Light described the formerly prosperous Selangor as "very Poor and almost deserted."[6]

The English country traders were suspicious of this Dutch activity. Francis Light had warned in 1784 that if the Dutch were victorious in their war with the Bugis, "they will destroy the ports of Rhio [Riau] and Selangore, and establish factories at these places and at Pera and Quedda [Kedah], which will entirely prevent any other nation from having a share in the trade of these countries, so far as to hinder them from bartering their opium and other goods for tin, pepper and other articles which are the produce of [these] countries, and so compel all other countries to deal with them [the Dutch] alone."[7]

Light's belief that the Dutch intended to close the Straits of Malacca to other Europeans, sometimes cited as a mere pretext to involve the English in a settlement in the Straits, was to be proved all too correct. By 1787 the VOC had moved into all the ports to the south of Malacca where an English settlement would have been feasible. Siak and Perak were "in alliance" with Malacca, and Riau, Selangor, Mempawah, and Sukadana in Kalimantan were "taken by the Dutch." Dutch factories had already existed in Palembang, Pontianak and Inderagiri. Light reported in 1786 that "The Dutch now possess both sides of the Straits of Malacca from the point Romania to the Latitude 5° North, nothing is left but the small kingdoms of Queda and Atjeh."[8] The Dutch had also taken steps to cut off all communication between the Straits of Malacca and Kalimantan. Even Trengganu and Perak, established VOC allies, experienced a toughening of Dutch attitudes during these years.[9]

The VOC was able to take this tough line because from 1784 it had at its disposal a naval force sent from Europe by the Netherlands State Government. Recognizing that the VOC's eastern holdings were of vital importance to the economic health of the state, the metropolitan government had been alarmed at the Company's inability to defend itself in the Anglo-Dutch war of 1780–84, and had sent reinforcements. The first of a series of government fleets, commanded by Admiral Jacob van Braam, had arrived at Malacca in June 1784, just in time to break the back of the Bugis siege.[10] The fleet's conquest of the flower of the Bugis forces made a lasting impression on the Malays and the Bugis.[11] The presence of this fleet, with a firepower far beyond that of the Malay or Bugis forces, totally changed the balance of power in the Straits. For years the local rulers had dealt with the Java-based VOC respectfully, but not subserviently. They had known the bounds of the VOC's interests in the Straits and its powers, and had defied Malacca confidently when they judged that Batavia would not be offended. They had been aware that the powers of the Dutch Company were waning. The arrival of van Braam's fleet seems to have completely confounded them. Dutch forward progress in the Straits after 1784 was swift and almost unchallenged.

But the fleet was only the means, not the cause of the most profound change in VOC policy in the Straits of Malacca in over a century. The most striking aspect of this second VOC war with the Bugis was that it was so obviously provoked by the Dutch themselves, in complete contradiction to the policies of strict neutrality towards the Bugis to which Batavia had held for so long. For over a century Batavia had counselled neutrality in Malay affairs. Financial prudence and hard-won experience had taught the VOC that there was no profit to be made in the Straits. In that area of many small ports and winding river systems, rival Asian and European traders had always found ways of circumventing any restrictions the Company attempted to place on the valuable tin, pepper, opium and cloth trades. These conditions had not changed. Moreover, the VOC was no longer primarily a trading company. It had become deeply entrenched in the agricultural economy of Java, and the risks of entering the trade of the Malacca Straits held little attraction. Nor had Batavia suddenly lost its aversion to the notion of a Malacca made rich by the passing trade. Batavia had no desire to promote a rival entrepôt. Stringent trade controls remained on both Riau and Malacca.[12] The extension of the VOC's power in the Malay world after 1784 was not an attempt to open doors, but, as Light and the other country traders had feared, to close them.

Malacca had been kept by the VOC not for its trade, but for its strategic importance, and it was for strategic, not commercial, reasons that the Dutch moved against the Bugis in 1784. The threat they perceived came not from the Bugis themselves, but from the English. For over a century the Dutch had expanded their sway in the Archipelago, free from any competition by a major European power. Now, the growing importance of the China tea trade to Europe, and the necessity of obtaining Archipelagan products—tin, pepper, spices—to exchange for tea in China had drawn the English East India Company's interest back to the Straits of Malacca. In the 1760s and 1770s the English had made several attempts to set up a base in the eastern seas. Various localities were tried; Balambangan in the Sulu Archipelago was actually settled briefly in 1773, and Aceh and Kedah were sounded out by Company agents in 1772.[13] But no agreement with the Malay rulers of these ports was achieved. Riau was the center of the English trade; sooner or later, English eyes must fall on the port. In 1784, Captain Thomas Forrest was en route to Riau with a proposal that an English settlement be established there when he received the news that the Dutch had overrun the port. He turned around, his mission unsuccessful.[14] The Dutch "forward movement" in the Straits after 1783 was an attempt to ensure, by bringing the Malay and Bugis rulers under the rule of the VOC, that no similar mission by the English to establish a post so close to the heart of Dutch interest in the Archipelago would succeed at any future date.

It was, to say the least, a policy full of risk, as Raja Haji's all too nearly successful siege of Malacca showed. The immediate risk was that the VOC would not be able to force its rule upon the Malay and Bugis princes. Jacob van Braam's fleet took care of that. But a further risk, perhaps even greater, lay in the possible response of the English. Batavia gambled that the English government would not wish, in time of peace, to provoke the Netherlands by meddling in areas that were, nominally at least, subject to the VOC.

In 1786 the growing protests of the country traders about the Dutch forward movement, allied to the real need for a base east of the Bay of Bengal, moved the English Company to commission Francis Light to establish a base at Penang, a dependency of Kedah to the north of Malacca. Paradoxically, news of the English occupation of Penang brought forth little response from the Dutch. Despite the obvious threat posed by Penang to Malacca's lucrative role as a provisioning port for the passing trade, there is little evidence in the Dutch correspondence that Batavia showed any great alarm at the English initiative. Dutch comments on the new British settlement were restricted to noting how this was affecting the price of tin and speculating—without any apparent urgency—that previous Dutch connections with Kedah might prove the English settlement invalid.[15] But that issue was not pushed. The simple fact is that Batavian officials knew they had little to fear from an English port at Penang.

Penang is situated well to the north of Malacca; any vessels coming from the Archipelago to the south with contraband goods could be diverted by patrol vessels stationed in the narrows between Malacca and Siak. It is notable that Penang, in its first decade, received very little tin from Bangka, (by then the VOC's main supplier of the mineral), in comparison to the large quantities which had flowed to Riau in the 1770s; and that trade to Penang from the eastern islands was negligible. Only one Bugis *perahu* reached Penang in 1787.[16] Malacca's trade did suffer, but the expostulations of the Malacca governor, Abraham Couperus, and others,[17] did nothing to stir the government at Batavia. It was perfectly aware of the losses to the Malaccan tin trade, and perfectly prepared to put up with them.

Riau, however, was still a different story. The English still eyed the port covetously, and had tried to persuade the Dutch government to release it to them in return for guarantees not to poach on established Dutch interests in the Archipelago.[18] But all their efforts had been in vain; the Dutch had no intention of losing control of Riau. When news arrived in Batavia in 1787 that the VOC garrison had been expelled from Riau by a group of mercenary Illanuns it caused a much greater stir than the news of the English settlement at Penang.

The expulsion of the Dutch garrison appears to have been an act of desperation on the part of the ruler of Riau, Sultan Mahmud of Johor. Cut off from the profitable country trade, Riau had rapidly lost its prosperity, and Sultan Mahmud had been unable to fulfill the financial obligations to the Dutch placed on him by the 1784 treaty. In February, 1787, Mahmud came to Malacca to sign a new convention to rectify this situation. This convention further eroded the Johor prince's independence, and greatly increased the powers of the Dutch Resident, David Rhudé.[19] Mahmud had been raised by the Bugis princes, and the double blow of being forced to renounce them, and the prosperity they had engendered, and to live under the thumb of the not-notably diplomatic Rhudé, was an unacceptable humiliation. "His Majesty Sultan Mahmud and the Raja Indera Bungsu were grief stricken and their sorrow was like a fire which consumed their discretion."[20] As his grandfather Sultan Sulaiman had before him, Mahmud called in a mercenary fleet to break his enemies' hold on Riau.[21] In 1787 a fleet of Illanun vessels from Tempassuk in northern Kalimantan sailed into the roads at Riau. With the surreptitious aid of Mahmud, the Illanuns attacked the Dutch garrison on the 13th of May. The garrison fled to Malacca, leaving Riau temporarily free of Dutch control.

But not for long. Orders were immediately issued from Batavia concerning the recovery and future defense of the port. The Batavian government declared that "for many serious reasons" Riau must not be abandoned, and that the garrison was to be strengthened to 200 European and 300 Asian soldiers. If the port could not be recaptured by the Company it must be totally destroyed, especially the harbor and anchorage.[22]

Sultan Mahmud did not stay to argue the point. Either out of fear of Dutch retaliation, or an inability to control the warlike Illanuns, he did not attempt to follow up his success. Soon after the flight of the Dutch garrison, Mahmud and the remaining Malay population also left Riau to settle on the island of Lingga, a little to the south. Without the Bugis, and with uncertain control of the Illanuns, Sultan Mahmud now in his turn sent an appeal to the English East India Company. He wrote in November, 1787, that the VOC had infringed his rights "as sole Sovereign of Rheo and Johore," embodied in his treaty with them of 1784, and appealed to the English Company to arbitrate this dispute, stipulating that they should come to his assistance if his allegations against the Dutch proved to be true.²³ The answer was an uncompromising refusal.

In the course of the two years, 1786–87, every Malay and Bugis prince (except Siak's, who had submitted to Batavia in the 1760s), had been pressed by the VOC into new and more comprehensive treaties, and had called on "their friends" the English to protect their independence. In 1786 Ibrahim of Selangor appealed to Light in Penang for large quantities of military stores and permission to hoist the English flag. He continued to press strongly for an English alliance through 1787.²⁴ Between 1785 and 1787 Raja Ali of Riau, Sultan Abdullah of Kedah, and Mahmud of Johor, all in turn approached the English; in 1787 Mansur Syah of Trengganu sent an ambassador first to Penang and then on to Calcutta, offering his pepper crop in exchange for opium from English traders. In the same year Malacca's ally, Perak, sought English protection against the Selangor fleet which menaced the Perak River.

All these rulers appealed naturally to the English, because their close, often personal, association with country traders such as Francis Light, Thomas Forrest, James Glass, and Robert Geddes had led them to believe that the English opposed the expansion of Dutch power in the area and were friendly to the smaller Malay communities. The extent of their confidence in the English can be seen in the perhaps incautious way the Sultan of Kedah allowed Light to settle Penang even before he had reached an explicit agreement with the English East India Company spelling out the terms of the arrangement.

He lived to regret it. When he finally realized that the English were not prepared to defend him against his enemies in return for the cession of Penang, and tried to rid himself of his unwelcome "guests," he received a rude shock. The English had no intention of withdrawing from Penang, and the Sultan had not the power to make them. In the end he was forced to live with the fact that he would receive no military support from the English, and that their new port at Penang was draining away all the trade which had previously favored Kedah. His alliance with the English had not only not strengthened his position, it had appreciably weakened it.[25]

None of the appeals made by the Malay or Bugis rulers for English aid met with the slightest success. To the English authorities in Calcutta, and even more to the Directorate and Board of Control in London, the tradition of Anglo-Dutch rivalry to which Light appealed, and from which the Malays and Bugis hoped to gain, was by the 1780s an anomaly. English interests in Europe dictated that the Dutch should be conciliated, to guard against their being driven even more deeply into the arms of the French, England's chief foe. Holland in league with France was too dangerous to English interests. Even after the signal English success against the Dutch in the 1780–84 war—perhaps because of this success—English interests required that the Netherlands be handled with kid gloves. Freedom of navigation of the Eastern seas, (one of the great gains of the recent war proclaimed by the Peace of Versailles in 1784), desirable though it undoubtedly was, was not to be obtained at the expense of further Anglo-Dutch discord. The key to its implementation was a sound base in the Archipelago; Riau would have been the best. But Riau was unobtainable. The Dutch were to be conciliated, not antagonized; where the VOC could and did lay claim to territory, the English withdrew.[26] European interests loomed far larger with the British government, and through them the government at Calcutta, than the needs of the Malay rulers and their allies, the country traders. The English East India Company's reply to the Raja Muda Raja Ali was a model of the official English policy. In it the acting Governor-General, John Macpherson, "warned Raja Ali that existing Anglo-Dutch treaties precluded British assistance to him."[27]

The Malays, whose chief contacts had been with the country traders, were totally unprepared for this attitude on the part of the English Company. Disappointed in his turn in expectations of English help after he had fled Riau in 1787, Sultan Mahmud of Johor made a desperate attempt to weld a coalition of Malay and Bugis forces against all Europeans in the Straits. But such a move had no real hope of success in view of the determination of the Dutch to control the ports of the Straits and their new willingness to commit forces to that end. Mahmud's rebellion was soon quelled, and the situation brought under control by the diplomacy of Governor Couperus of Malacca. Perhaps the attempted coalition was merely a face-saving contrivance by Sultan Mahmud, allowing him at last to take the only course left and seek reconciliation with the Dutch. Couperus was aware of the delicacy of Malay pride in such a situation, and he used his knowledge well, providing the Malay rulers with acceptable ways to make their peace with the VOC. By 1795 only Sultan Mahmud, who had helped expel the garrison from Riau, still labored under the disfavor of the Dutch; and that year both he and the Bugis leader Raja Ali arrived at an understanding with the Company.[28]

For the first time in a century-and-a-half of occupation of Malacca, the VOC was truly dominant in the Straits.

NOTES

1. Thomas Forrest, an employee of the English East India Co., was on his way to Riau with orders to establish a post from which free trade might be opened "not only with the Inhabitants of Rhio, but of all the Neighbouring Islands," when he discovered it had fallen to the Dutch. Bassett, "British Commercial and Strategic Interest in the Malay Peninsula," 138.

2. Netscher, *Djohor*, 209–11. See also Raja Ali Haji ibn Ahmad, *The Precious Gift*, 179, 187–88; Bassett, "Anglo-Malay Relations," 192, 195.

3. Kol. Arch. 3594, C. G. Baumgarten's Report (9 May 1785).

4. Sultan Ibrahim to Macpherson (June 1785) cited in Bassett, "Anglo-Malay Relations," 191.

5. "During this period rice was expensive in Selangor . . . and this was also true of all other foodstuffs." Raja Ali Haji ibn Ahmad, *The Precious Gift*, 183.

6. Cited in H. P. Clodd, *Malaya's First British Pioneer*, 158.

7. SSR, 1. Light to Andrew Ross (1784): 150.

8. SSR, 1. Light to Macpherson (25 January 1786.) Cited in Harlow, *The Founding of the Second British Empire*, 2: 349.

9. Tin was to be delivered to VOC at old (1773) price of 32 rds. "During the following months Sultan Alauddin (of Perak) was forced to accept a number of instructions from Melaka which would have aroused immediate objections from either of his brothers." B. Andaya, *Perak*, 360.

10. van Papendrecht, 22.

11. The name of the commander of the fleet, Jacob van Braam, is cited time after time in the *Tuhfat*, often in places where he was completely uninvolved—far more often than that of any other European. See Raja Ali Haji ibn Ahmad, *The Precious Gift*, index.

12. Soon after the conquest of Riau the Malacca governor, Gerardus de Bruijn, pointed out that if the VOC wanted to profit from their military success they must open Riau or Malacca to the European trade; otherwise another Asian port would soon appear to service this trade. Harrison, "Trade in the Straits of Malacca in 1785," 57, 61. A. E. van Braam Houckgeest and the next Governor of Malacca, Abraham Couperus, also submitted arguments for such a policy. See J. de Hullu's, "A. E. Van Braam Houckgeest's Memorie over Malakka en den Tinhandel aldaar (1790)," *BKI* 76 (1920): 284–309, and "De Engelschen op Poeloe Pinang en de Tinhandel der Oost-Indische Compagnie (VOC) in 1788," (A Memorie by Gov. Abraham Couperus 13 September 1788) *BKI* 77 (1921): 605–14. Batavia remained unimpressed.

13. Ibid. 127.

14. Bassett, "British Commercial and Strategic Interest," 138.

15. Kol. Arch. 3704, Generale Missiven (30 December 1788): 4062.

16. Bassett, "Anglo-Malay Relations," 195.

17. See note 14 above.

18. Tarling, *Anglo-Dutch Rivalry*, 3–50.

19. Netscher, Djohor, 206–09.

20. Raja Ali Haji ibn Ahmad, *The Precious Gift*, 184. "The agent in Riau wanted everything done immediately, harshly demanding whatever he wanted."

21. Ibid. 185.

22. van der Chijs, *Realia*, 2:191.

23. Bassett, "Anglo-Malay Relations," 197.

24. Ibid. 195.

25. Ibid. 204–10.

26. Tarling, *Anglo-Dutch Rivalry*, 23–46.

27. Bassett, "Anglo-Malay Relations" 192.

28. Ibid. 203.

CONCLUSION

On the 14th of January, 1795, Governor Couperus celebrated 154 years of Dutch rule of Malacca. Couperus might have felt a pardonable satisfaction in his government's accomplishments. He had successfully negotiated peace with all the surrounding rulers, even Sultan Mahmud of Johor; no strong Malay port had succeeded Riau as a center for the passing and local trade. Trust in the English was at an all-time low among the Malays after the failure of the East India Company to come to the aid of the various Malay rulers in the 1780s; and the English Company seemed content with their establishment at Penang, too far to the north of Malacca to attract trade from within the Archipelago. There must have seemed no good reason why Malacca should not remain in Dutch hands for another 154 years, and the English be kept at bay to the north for all that period.

But Malacca's success in the 1780s was built on decisions made in The Hague and London, not Batavia. European power had made itself felt earlier in the Malay world than in other areas in Southeast Asia, perhaps because of the very nature of that world. This was not an isolated, self-contained agricultural society, but a bustling, outgoing trading community, necessarily keyed to look outward, and, therefore, necessarily influenced by outside events. European politics mattered to Malay princes as they did not to others, for by the late eighteenth century

Europeans dominated a significant fraction of the international trade which had always been the life-blood of the Malay establishment. When the metropolitan government in the Netherlands decided to take a hand in the East to protect their interests and sent a series of fleets to the Indies, the Malay powers were faced with a formidable force; one which apparently overwhelmed them completely. For the first time in over a century the VOC was in a position to enforce its will in the Straits of Malacca.

But by 1795 a new game was afoot in Europe; the Napoleonic Wars had broken out. Previous policies were toppled with little thought to local consequences. In August, on the authority of the Kew Letters and at the behest of a Stadtholder, who had taken refuge in England from the upheavals of the Continent, Governor Abraham Couperus surrendered the still formidable fortress of Malacca to an English force with barely a shot fired.[1]

Dutch occupation of Malacca effectively ended when Governor Couperus surrendered the fortress. Much had changed by the time the Dutch returned, briefly, to the Peninsula in 1818. The French were for the time being no longer a force to be reckoned with. English power in India had been consolidated and strengthened, and the trade to China was growing ever more important. The great Company that had guided Dutch fortunes in the East since 1606, had died with the eighteenth century; and the even older stone fortress of Malacca, a potent symbol of European power in the Malay world for almost three centuries, had died with it, demolished from within by British explosives.

Within a year of the Dutch return there was to be an even greater change. In 1819 the English established a new settlement at Singapore, south of Malacca. Balked of Riau by the Dutch, they had found a substitute. The important difference was, whereas Riau had been the center of a flourishing Malay polity, the home of a ruler of an old, established lineage, Singapore was a backwater. The port which grew there had no real links to any Malay ruler of consequence. The new entrepôt, which quickly outstripped Riau, or even Malacca in its heyday, as the volume of trade through the Straits continued to swell yearly, was a British, not a Malay port. The role of the Malay ruler was entirely nominal, and the traffic which flowed through of the Malacca Straits in the nineteenth century, though greater than ever before, nourished no traditional Malay polity.

Once Singapore was established, and the Dutch realized that no amount of protest on their part would persuade the English to part with it, Malacca lost all significance to the Dutch. They handed it over, and with it their interests in the Malay Peninsula, to the English in 1824 in return for guarantees that their interests in Sumatra would be respected.[2] Bangka and Palembang, which they retained, produced much more tin than Perak. Riau remained in the Dutch sphere of influence, but with the foundation of Singapore most of its importance had evaporated. Singapore represented what the Dutch had most feared—a free port following in the footsteps of Malay Malacca, a foreign European power firmly based right on the threshold of their sphere of influence in the Archipelago.

But it also represented, as Aceh and Johor had in times past, an ally within the Straits capable of warding off further foreign encroachment and helping to maintain the security of the international trade route. Paradoxically, the Malaccan outpost was made unnecessary by the very eventuality it had been maintained to prevent. With the powerful English now established in Singapore and still keen to maintain an alliance with them, the Dutch no longer had any need to keep a garrison in Malacca to protect their empire in Java and the eastern Archipelago.

Malacca had not flourished in its 154 years of Dutch rule. By the early eighteenth century this once bustling international entrepôt could be described as "a place of no great trade."[3] Any hopes the rulers of the VOC had entertained of channelling the trade of the Straits to their own benefit began and ended with the dismal failure of their attempts to control the Indian trade in the 1650s. This was enough to prove the futility of any attempt to monopolize trade in such an intricate and widespread area, with so many possible ports and such a highly mobile population. Moreover, as early as 1641 commentators were pointing out the divergence of interest between Batavia and Malacca. Inevitably, given the power structure of the Company, Batavia won. In the 1660s the administration at Batavia contemplated destroying the northern port completely—they would hardly have withdrawn from the post and left the fortress intact. Traditional strategic wisdom prevailed, and the old city remained garrisoned, but often feebly and to little effect. The Malaccan government never commanded a force of more than 600 soldiers and a ragtag collection of vessels quite insufficient to act against all but the weakest of the local powers.

Far from seeking to dominate the area, Batavia became actively involved in the Straits only when the security of Malacca itself was at risk. They sent reinforcements in the mid-1720s when the growing power of the Bugis menaced Malacca, and again in 1758 when the town was besieged and in danger of falling into Bugis hands. The reluctance of Batavia to act in the face of what Malaccan governors saw as real threats to the interest of the Company (as in 1714 when Johor appeared about to become a major Malay power), and the central government's complaisance in the face of Malay "smuggling" ports—even Riau in the 1760s and 1770s—bespeaks indifference to the area and its trade. Batavia's interest had always lain elsewhere, in the Moluccas and Macassar, its own hinterland in Java, not in the uncontrollable north. Even the security of the passage of the Straits to India had become of minor importance to the VOC after the dwindling of their trade with Malabar at the end of the seventeenth century.

The exception which proved the rule was the capture of Riau in 1784, and the subsequent Dutch determination to maintain their control of the port. At first glance this was in total contradiction to their previous policy. Closer examination explains the paradox. Dutch interest in Riau was aroused by their fear not of the Bugis, but of the English. The determination of the Dutch to suppress Riau arose from their knowledge that the English Company was seriously interested in establishing a base in the port, a base which, linked with the Archipelago-wide trade network of the Bugis, would have given them access to the produce of the whole of the Archipelago. The VOC would probably have acted even earlier if it had had the power, but that only became available with the advent of van Braam's fleet in 1784. Significantly, no attempt was made to benefit commercially from the fall of Riau, despite the pleas of successive Malaccan governors. The aggressive policies which marked the last decade of Dutch rule of Malacca only emphasize the fact that they saw the area as an outpost necessary to protect their interests in the Archipelago itself, not as an asset in its own right. Malacca was of peripheral importance to the VOC, and treated accordingly.

So much, then, for the significance of Dutch Malacca to the VOC. What of its significance to the Malay polities? Does my study bear out

J. C. van Leur's famous statement that "any talk of a European Asia in the eighteenth century is out of the question?"[4] Here the story is less clear. The climate of the Indonesian Archipelago, both political and physical, has been inimical to historical research. Primary Malay sources have not survived, and the Dutch documentation is of limited application to Malay politics. But the Dutch letters do allow us some glimpses of the contemporary Malay world, and, I believe, allow us to come to some conclusions about it.

Certainly van Leur was correct in his dismissal of the concept of an "effete and decaying" Asian world in the eighteenth century. "It seems to me" he wrote, "inaccurate to dispose of such Indonesian states as Palembang, Siak, Achin, or Johore with the qualifications corrupt despotism, pirate states, and slave states, hotbeds of political danger and decay."[5] There is no indication in a reading of the correspondence between Malacca and Batavia that the Malay and Bugis communities were in any way decayed and lacking in direction. Leaders of the stature of the Raja Muda Mahmud of Johor, Sultan Muhammad Jiwa of Kedah, Raja Kecik of Siak, Mansur Syah of Trengganu, or the Bugis from Daeng Parani to Raja Haji, did not spring from an effete or decadent society. They dealt with Dutch Malacca with scant respect, and certainly held the government there in no especial awe. If they displayed more circumspection in their dealings with Batavia, it was only to the extent that one would have expected in their dealing with any powerful Javanese state.

Nevertheless, without disrespect to van Leur and to the generation of post-colonial historians who embraced his ideas, I would argue that, in their desire to redress the balance in favor of autonomous Asian history, they are too ready to dismiss the *effect* of the Dutch occupation of Malacca on its neighbors. A century-and-a-half of Dutch presence in Malacca left its mark on Malay society in an important way, and was highly destructive to one aspect of Malay society—the political structure.

The pre-industrial Malay polity was a delicately balanced, demographically unstable structure based on wealth,[6] and that wealth, in this area of poor soil and shifting populations, was drawn largely from the passing international trade. Thus, the basis of any powerful Malay state which would have been capable of facing and dealing with the wave of technically superior European encroachment that was to come in the early nineteenth century (in the way that the Thai state did) had to be based on a large, central entrepôt or harbor principality, such as Malay Malacca. When the Chinese revived their trade to the Straits in the fifteenth century, they understood the need for a strong local power to ensure the peace and security of the area, and in their wisdom encouraged the ruler of Malacca in his aspirations. The Portuguese, on the contrary, imagined that they could capture the wealth of Asia by force alone, and drove the Malay court out of Malacca. This did not necessarily mean the end of the possibility of a strong Malay central power; new centers arose in Aceh and Johor, to draw trade from Portuguese Malacca. But the trade was splintered, and the struggle to recapture it shook the Straits for over a century, till the Dutch, in alliance with Johor, drove out the Portuguese in 1641.

The Dutch were at first glance far less destructive of the Malay polities than the Portuguese. They did not openly challenge the Malay rulers, as the Portuguese had done. They did not in practice make any claim to overlordship; by the eighteenth century, they had even come to see the benefits to themselves of the existence of a strong Malay power capable of policing the Straits, and their alliance with Johor helped it to an ascendency over Aceh, so that for the first time since 1511 a single Malay power dominated the Straits. But the Dutch had no intention of giving up their outpost at Malacca, and they expected it at least to attempt to pay its own way. They appear never to have appreciated the dynamic at the base of Malay politics: the need to control absolutely, by force if necessary, the trade of the Straits. (No more did the Englishman Thomas Stamford Raffles, apparently, when he set up an English port in Singapore to siphon off the international trade from the Malay polities and then wrote of them as "decayed".) Even when Batavia stayed completely neutral in Malay affairs, by their very presence at Malacca the Dutch inhibited the growth of any centralized Malay power.

The old states, Srivijaya and Malacca, had depended on their predominance as trade centers as much on as their sea-power to control their subjects. The presence in the Straits of a foreign port, free of the needs of a hinterland and protected by a foreign power (Batavia), operated strongly against the interests of all those Malay rulers who sought to assert their power over more than a small portion of the Malay world. As early as the 1670s Malaccan Governor Balthasar Bort, lured by the newly discovered tin of the upper Siak river, made an accord with the traders of Patupahan. That this accord was not recognized by the ruler of Johor was obvious from Governor Bort's Report and the less partial comments of traders such as William Dampier. Johor made a determined but unsuccessful attempt to put an end to this trade; but the revenues had become too important for Malacca to give the trade up, and it played a large and irritating part in Dutch relations with Johor for the next half century. It is not unrealistic to suggest that the weakness shown by the continued loss of the Siak revenue to Malacca—and the inability to control a rebellious portion of the population—might have played a part in the subsequent fall of the Laksamana in the mid-1680s.

Again, when the Bendahara family sought to assert Johor's ascendancy as the premier Malay power in the early eighteenth century, Malacca was to play a highly significant though seemingly innocuous part in the events which led to the collapse of Johor in 1718. Despite the dislocation caused by the loss of the old Malacca line and the disaffection of many Malay communities, the Raja Muda Mahmud's power grew rapidly until he tried to impress his overlordship on the immigrant Bugis settlers of Selangor. Here he met humiliating defeat, his forces being repulsed on several occasions. But why was it necessary for Johor, a sea power, to face the well-known prowess of the Bugis warriors on land at all? Would it not have been easier for the Raja Muda to surround the port and cut off supplies to the Bugis? True, they could have travelled inland; but would it have been feasible to ship provisions and munitions overland from Perak, a port of little consequence at that date, or Kedah, with whom they were on dubious terms? The distances were great, the terrain daunting.

But Malacca—within reach by land, totally outside the Raja Muda's control because of his demonstrated reluctance to quarrel with Batavia, hungry for the tin that could be produced in Selangor far more easily than rice or other foodstuffs—Malacca was the force which kept the Bugis alive at the beginning of their conflict with the Raja Muda of Johor. Malacca, smarting under the rebuffs and disdainful treatment so recently meted out to it by Johor, desperate to satisfy the heavy demands of its masters in Batavia for tin, was only too ready to ignore the complaints coming from Riau that in accommodating the Bugis they were materially opposing Johor. And the Dutch at Malacca were not, in their light, overstepping the bounds of neutrality; they did not ally themselves with the Bugis, they sent no troops, did not even let the Bugis settle on VOC territory; they did not even (at least officially) allow the Bugis to buy munitions; but they bought the Bugis' tin, and thus supplied them with the most valuable weapon in the arsenal of a Malay state; trade. Without Malacca, the Bugis would have had little chance of survival against an opponent such as Johor.

The pattern repeats itself in Siak. Again and again Malacca encouraged the people of Siak to look to it, rather than to Johor, as a market for their tin and other products. From the 1670s on the struggle to control the Siak trade is a constant theme of the Malacca government. Here the Malaccan Dutch were actively involved in wooing the trade away from Johor. Even Raja Kecik was unable to force the Siak merchants to accept his right to control their trade with Malacca.

Thus all Johor's continuing efforts to heal itself of internal strife broke on the rock of the Dutch presence in Malacca. There were other major crises and dislocations; the loss of the old Malacca line in 1699, the enmity caused by the immigration of Bugis and Minangkabau groups. But dynasties have come and gone, and strong rulers, or their descendents, have a way of developing their own mystique in the wake of success. As for the immigrants, such groups would have surely been a strength to a strong and properly functioning Malay ruler; the nature of Malay society was such that it had always absorbed such newcomers quite readily. I am not trying to argue that these matters were not of major importance in the context of eighteenth-century Malay politics; but that, given time, and the natural course of events, they would have been overcome.

But the natural course of events was what the Dutch presence in Malacca denied. The last attempt to establish a powerful Malay polity came with the growth of Riau as a Bugis entrepôt for the English country trade. Riau, as the port for a Johor ruled by an acknowledged scion of an old Malay line—the Bendahara dynasty had achieved respectability with time—and reinforced with the economic and military power of the Bugis, was a force to be reckoned with. Would Raffles, one wonders, have found the inhabitants of Riau "effete" and "decayed"? Forrest, Light, and the other country traders of the 1760s and 1770s, not to mention the Dutch, certainly did not. But Riau too ran aground on the rock of Malacca. In this, perhaps, Raja Haji, who led the siege, was unlucky; his siege might even have succeeded, if it had not been for the arrival of van Braam's fleet. Still, it was conflict with the Dutch forces in Malacca which had caused his downfall.

In this way the seventeenth and eighteenth centuries saw a fragmentation of the Malay political world, though it was an extremely gradual process, driven by external rather than internal circumstances. The period did not give rise to any decrease in its economic activity, or in the vitality of its society in general. Certainly the Malaccan government never ceased to consider its Malay neighbors with respect—only consider Governor de Bruijn's warnings that the Malay rulers would soon set up a new port if the Dutch did not fill the gap themselves. Riau does appear to have regained a degree of prosperity after the Dutch garrison left, to the extent that the interim English government of Malacca sent William Farquhar in 1818 to negotiate an accord with the ruler, Raja Muda Raja Jafar. But Raja Jafar, the son of Raja Haji, was perhaps not unnaturally nervous of English promises to defend him against future Dutch resentments;[7] and when the Dutch came back to Riau in 1818 to reclaim their rights he submitted to them without calling on his new "allies."[8] It was left to that brilliant student of Malay politics, Thomas Stamford Raffles, to fish in the troubled waters of continuing Malay-Bugis enmity, and procure an alternate site for an English entrepôt from the more acquiescent—and less powerful—Malay prince, Tengku Lung, a son of the late Sultan Mahmud.[9]

Would the story have been different if Raffles had been confronted by a single, wealthy Malay polity, ruled by the like of the Malay Raja Muda Mahmud? History is not a matter of "what if"s; it is a matter of why, and how, and what. In an area such as the Straits these questions are not easy to answer. The jungle soon swallows up the past; the Malay world of the eighteenth century remains almost as much terra incognita to us now as it was when van Leur first wrote. I have tried to cast a little light into the dark areas by looking over the shoulders, as it were, of the adventurers who came there from northern Europe. The view is often constricted, the patterns unclear; but enough can be seen to show that the period was more than just an unimportant phase in Malay history, that it contained its heroes and heroines, its crises and moments of decision in full measure. The eighteenth century was critical in the shaping of the modern Malay political structure. It was not a time of European domination, nor of Malay isolation or decadence. It was a time when the Malay polities faced a new world, a world where no area was to be left in isolation, where actions taken in one country were to have significant repercussions half way around the globe; a modern, industrialized world. And because of the presence of the Dutch port of Malacca in their midst, they were to face it in disunity.

NOTES

1. Graham Irwin, "Governor Couperus and the Surrender of Malacca, 1795," *JMBRAS* 29.3 (1956): 86–133; Bassett, "The Surrender of Dutch Malacca," *BKI* 117.3 (1961): 344–45.

2. Tarling, *Anglo-Dutch Rivalry,* 133.

3. Lockyer, *An Account of the Trade in India,* 66.

4. J. C. van Leur, *Indonesian Trade and Society,* 274.

5. Ibid. 276.

6. "Malays, it would seem, sought wealth not for its own sake but as a means for gaining political influence in the form of a sizable personal following." A. C. Milner, *KERAJAAN; Malay Political Culture on the Eve of Colonial Rule,* 27. See also 20ff.

7. Raja Ali Haji ibn Ahmad, *The Precious Gift,* 223–24.

8. Tarling, *Anglo Dutch Rivalry,* 92. See also Raja Ali Haji ibn Ahmad, *The Precious Gift,* 386.

9. Ibid. 226–29.

Appendix I

MALACCA'S GOVERNORS, 1641–1795

Johan van Twist	1641–1642
Jeremias van Vliet	1642–1645
Arnold de Vlaming van Oudshoorn	1645–1646
Jan Thijsen Payart	1646–1662
Jan van Riebeeck	1662–1665
Balthasar Bort	1665–1677
Jacob Jorizoon Pits*	1677–1680
Cornelis van Quallberg	1680–1684
Nicolaas Schag(h)en	1684–1685
Francois Tack	1685
Thomas Slicher	1686–1691
Gelmer Vosburgh	1692–1696
Goveert van Hoorn	1696–1700
Bernard Phoonsen	1700–1704
Johan Grotenhuijs*	1704
Carol Bolnar	1704–1706
Pieter Rooselaar	1706–1709
Willem Six	1710–1711
Willem Moerman	1711–1717
Hermanus van Suchtelen*	1717–1727
Johan Frederick Gobius	1727–1730
Pieter Rochus Pasques de Chavonnes	1731–1736

* Served previously at Malacca in a subordinate position.

David Johan Bake	1735
Rogier de Laver	1736–1743
Willem Bernard Albinus*	1743–1749
Pierter van Heemskerk*	1749–1753
Willem Dekker	1754–1758
David Boelen	1758–1764
Thomas Schippers	1764–1772
Jan Crans	1772–1777
Pieter Geradus de Bruijn	1777–1788
Abraham Couperus*	1788–1795

* Served previously at Malacca in a subordinate position.

Appendix II

PROFITS AND LOSSES[1]

Year	Income	Expenditure	Profit	Loss
1641–42				49312.19. 9
1642–43				79945.15. 0
1643–44				
1644–45				
1645–46				
1646–47	172901. 1.11	210866.13. 1		37966. 0. 0
1647–48				
1648–49	161732.12.14	195159. 0.10		33427. 0. 0
1649–50				
1650–51				
1651–52				

1. These are raw figures for profit and loss at Malacca according to the VOC's calculations, drawn from the archives of the VOC, held at the Rijksarchief, The Hague. The annual figures for profit and loss were usually included in one or other of the letters from Malacca to Batavia each year. Where that source has not been available for a particular year, I have drawn wherever possible on the figures sent in the Generale Missiven from Batavia to The Netherlands, a summary of the year's events in the East drawn up annually by the Batavian Council for the Metropolitan authorities. The gaps—except in Profit where there was an overall Loss, or vice versa—indicate years where I have not been able to locate any figures in either of these sources.

The amounts listed are Dutch guilders.

Year	Income	Expenditure	Profit	Loss
1652–53				96262.17. 1
1653–54	151788. 6. 6	195150.13. 8		43362. 0. 0
1654–55	171777. 0. 0	242659. 0. 0		70882. 0. 0
1655–56				66911.14.13
1656–57	114360. 3. 0	207838.16. 0		93478. 0. 0
1657–58	134523. 4. 4	243880.11. 0		109357. 0. 0
1658–59	167056.17. 2	258029. 6. 1		90973. 0. 0
1659–60				
1660–61	.			49042.13. 8
1661–62				
1662–63				96623.12. 9
1663–64				47852. 3.15
1664–65			3846. 0. 3	
1665–66				68715.18. 1
1666–67	201013. 9. 0	187033.14. 1	20627.14. 3	
1667–68			30604. 7.15	
1668–69				
1669–70				
1670–71	229316. 2. 9	192392. 5.13	43643. 0. 5	
1671–72	251011. 5. 0	171671.12.14		
1672–73	212793. 8. 9	187877. 2.13	19535.16. 3	
1673–74				
1674–75			2432.12. 0	
1675–76	22388. 1.10	189063.17.15	32329. 2. 3	
1676–77	184539.15. 0	188345.10. 4		10774.17. 4
1677–78				92672. 1.14
1678–79				41091. 0. 6
1679–80				32651.17.10
1680–81			17217. 0. 0	
1681–82				21118.14. 2
1682–83	38432.19. 3	29010. 7.11		34543.14. 1
1683–84				57398. 0. 0
1684–85				15292. 0. 0
1685–86				46310. 0. 0
1686–87				
1687–88	143175. 0. 0	167112. 0. 0		

Year	Income	Expenditure	Profit	Loss
1688–89			52710. 0. 0	
1689–90				
1690–91				74244. 0. 0
1691–92	84308. 0. 0	147064. 0. 0		
1692–93				
1693–94				
1694–95				
1695–96				
1696–97				
1697–98	65595. 0. 0	123701. 0. 0		
1698–99				
1699–00	58669. 0. 0	109693. 0. 0		
1700–01	52245. 6. 8	121870. 1. 8		69624.15. 0
1701–02	53929.13. 8	135719. 1. 8		81790. 9. 8
1702–03				
1703–04	36927.14. 0	150590. 7. 8		113662.13. 8
1704–05	52590.18. 0	163220.12. 8		110629.14. 8
1705–06	235919. 3. 0	142759.13. 0	93183.10. 0[2]	
1706–07	58079.17. 8	146275.10. 0		88196.12. 8
1707–08				
1708–09	126713. 1. 0	141933. 1. 6		15220.15. 0
1709–10	70528. 5. 0	157984. 6. 0		87456. 1. 0
1710–11	83017. 1. 8	160028. 6. 8		77045. 5. 0
1711–12	101416. 3. 0	138272. 9. 0		36856. 0. 0
1712–13	141335.17. 8	155695. 1. 8		14359. 4. 0
1713–14	72736. 9. 0	131532.11. 8		58796. 2. 8
1714–15	64613.14. 8	133133.13. 0		68519.18. 8
1715–16	75403. 7. 8	125307. 8. 8		49904. 1. 0
1716–17	82025.09. 0	131246.12. 8		49221. 3. 8
1717–18	93647. 3. 0	134999. 0. 0		41352. 0. 0
1718–19	71283. 0. 0	133608. 5. 8		62327. 5. 0
1719–20	88172. 0. 0	136371.13. 0		48199.13. 0
1720–21	103861. 5. 8	155530.19. 8		51669.14. 0

2. The *Generale Missiven* comments that these are the first real profits since 1676; 1680–81 and 1688–89 were merely "boekingsbedragen" [acounting-figures—not actual profits].

Year	Income	Expenditure	Profit	Loss
1721–22	69195. 4. 8	142587.17. 0		73392.12. 8
1722–23	95661.12. 8	172601. 6. 0		76939.13. 8
1723–24	92621. 4. 0	158084.19. 0		65463.15. 0
1724–25	113255. 4. 0	153652. 7. 8		40397. 6. 8
1725–26	60159. 5. 8	142546. 0. 8		82386.15. 0
1726–27	132888.14. 8	143818. 0. 0		10929. 5. 8
1727–28	77883.13. 8	150123.15. 8		72240. 2. 0
1728–29	80314.10. 8	149048.17. 0		68734. 6. 8
1729–30	63840. 0. 0	155319.15. 8		92869.16. 8
1730–31	46831.19. 8	146614. 4. 8		99782.15. 0
1731–32	130501. 0. 0	167743. 4. 8		37242. 4. 8
1732–33	94918. 3. 0	151763.10. 8		56845.07.08
1733–34	1000747.12. 0	161353.13. 8		60606. 1. 8
1734–35	67026.19. 0	145559. 4. 0		78532.05. 0
1735–36	132968. 4. 0	138955. 7. 0		5987. 5. 0
1736–37	58072. 4. 8	150605.14. 0		92533. 9. 0
1737–38	138814.12. 0	157687.18. 8		18872.18. 8
1738–39	75012. 5. 8	146847.10. 8		71834.15. 0
1739–40	122875.07.08	156257. 7. 8		33382. 0. 0
1740–41	144083. 4. 0	156129.19. 8		12046. 5. 8
1741–42	82692.17. 0	153555. 0. 0		70862.15. 8
1742–43	109974. 4. 0	141685. 2. 8		31710.18. 8
1743–44	69234.16. 8	123667.16. 8	54433. 0. 0	
1744–45	9526.10. 0	120969.18. 8		25723. 8. 8
1745–46	122694.17. 0	130062. 0. 0		7367. 9. 8
1746–47	108762. 4. 8	118785. 3. 0		10022.18. 8
1747–48	111996.15. 0	121038. 4. 8		9041. 9. 8
1748–49	99590. 5. 0	118797.16. 8		19207.11. 8
1749–50	87856.15. 8	125181. 7. 8		37324.12. 0
1750–51	103213. 9. 8	178282. 5. 0		75068. 5. 8
1751–52	118513.12. 0	142434.18. 8		23921. 6. 8
1752–53	133362.12. 8	141214. 8. 8		7851.16. 0
1753–54	144321. 6. 0	122321. 6. 0	21511. 0. 0	
1754–55	111534.19. 0	175075.10. 8		63540.11. 8
1755–56	104519. 1. 8	198486.15. 0		93967.13. 8
1756–57		235984.12. 0		

Year	Income	Expenditure	Profit	Loss
1757–58				
1758–59	115924. 7. 8	168384.13. 0		52424. 5. 8
1759–60				
1760–61	117486.18. 8	192252. 5. 0		74765. 6. 8
1761–62	96166.11. 0	136485.14. 0		40321. 3. 0
1762–63	100298. 9. 8	131094.01. 8		30795.11. 0
1763–64	104309.19.08	114313. 5. 0		10003. 5. 8
1764–65		114057. 9. 0		
1765–66	131695. 9. 0	121331. 0. 0	10364. 9. 0	
1766–67	140990.14. 0	167152.18. 8		36526.13. 9
1767–68	147610.19. 8	163645.17. 0		16034.17. 8
1768–69	120473. 6. 0	116618.12. 8	3854.13. 8	
1769–70	124833.16. 0	121628. 3. 0	3205.13. 0	
1770–71		116843.12. 0		
1771–72	150652.16.00	138420.11. 8	12234. 4. 8	
1772–73	160818.16. 0	123830. 8. 0	12234. 8. 0	
1773–74	188553.11. 8	122417.18. 0	66135.13. 8	
1774–75	210767. 2. 0	129777.11. 8	80989.10. 8	
1775–76	168176.12. 0	127509. 1. 8	40667.11. 0	
1776–77	178312.14. 0	127523. 7. 0		
1777–78	183522. 9. 0	117455. 0. 0	66067. 9. 0	
1778–79	164152. 1. 8	113235.10. 0	50889.11.8	
1779–80	162396.16. 8	112613. 1. 8	49783.15. 0	
1780–81	140666. 9. 0	131374.19. 8	9291. 9. 8	
1781–82				
1782–83	150017.14. 0	144130. 6. 0	5887. 8. 0	
1783–84				
1784–85	204206.19. 8	320808.15. 8		116301.16. 0
1785–86	342308. 0. 0	428088. 7. 8		85780. 6. 8
1786–87	290943.17. 0	360976. 3. 0		
1787–88	255597.19. 0	472639. 8. 0		
1788–89	225671.13. 8	389639.11. 0		163967.17. 8
1789–90	244662.12. 0	385575. 8. 0		140912.12. 0

Appendix III

MALACCA'S FREEBURGHERS

Malacca's freeburghers were residents of Malacca, subjects but not employees of the VOC. They were generally of European extraction, often descendents of the old Portuguese families that had intermarried with local families of similar rank, or previous employees of the VOC who had earned the right to settle in VOC territory. They never played as large a role in Dutch trade in Asia as their counterparts had under the Portuguese. Officially, their trade was severely limited by the Company. They were allowed to deal only in items of little or no interest to the VOC.

Malacca freeburghers traded to Sumatra, especially to the Siak River, and the Peninsula (in 1678 they were permitted to trade only to Batavia, Johor, Pahang, Riau, Rio Formosa, Muar, Kelang, Kedah, Perak, Asahan, Kampar, Siak, Ujung Salang and Bangkeri), carrying jungle goods and fish products from Sumatra and distributing foodstuffs such as rice, salt, and cane sugar brought from Siam or Java.[1] They could sell cloth bought from the VOC or at public auction in Malacca, and could buy tin and gold on condition that it be delivered to the Company in Malacca. In this role they were useful as retail traders of the Company's imports.

The restrictions on the extent of their voyages were eased somewhat in the 1740s under the reforms of Governor-General Van Imhoff. He aimed to withdraw the Company from the smaller sectors of inter-Asian trade, where it could not compete with independent operators, and to open such areas of trade to residents in the Company's establishments. Van Imhoff believed that the Company would profit from the tolls and duties of an increased independent trade. However, such trade was still to be restricted, as each voyage must originate and terminate at Batavia, and the Malacca freeburghers did not greatly benefit from the concessions.[2] Of course the freeburghers circumvented the VOC's restrictions as often as possible, as English country traders visiting Malacca frequently noted.[3]

The vessels of these freeburghers were often employed by Malaccan officials to supplement their never adequate fleet, for sending dispatches, collecting cargo, or blockading the Malay ports when necessary. In 1728 this fleet amounted to twenty-seven small vessels; in 1732 this number had fallen to fifteen, and in 1737 to twelve. Tolls from the trade of the freeburghers did play an important part in the domestic economy of the port of Malacca, as the Malaccan government's dismay at Raja Mahmud's attempts to close down the burgher trade to Siak in 1710 demonstrates.

After 1670 duty collected on their trade to Siak and Bangkalis formed a vital portion of Malacca's revenue, and Malaccan governments were particularly protective of their rights for this reason.

NOTES

1. van der Chijs, *Plakaatboek*, 3 (1678): 10.
2. Dampier, *Voyages,* 114; and Lockyer, *Account*, 67.
3. Hall, *History of Southeast Asia,* 312.

Glossary

anak raja	of royal blood
bahar	main unit of weight; about 375 Dutch lbs, or 400 English lbs
bendahara	first minister in a Malay court
chiap	seal
daulat	majesty; mysterious kingly power which does not die with a ruler
Daeng	a Bugis title of distinction
derhaka	treason
freeburghers	European free-born residents of VOC ports, subjects of the Company. See Appendix III
Kalimantan	Borneo
laksamana	Minister in a Malay court corresponding to a minister of Marine or admiral
lastpost	unprofitable post [Dutch]
Moors	Dutch term for Muslim traders from India
memorie	(Dutch.) Memorandum. The report left by the governor of an outpost at the termination of his office.
nachoda	captain of a trading vessel
negari	Malay state or settlement
orang kaya; orang kaya besar	rich men, notables; men of substance
orang laut	men of the sea
perahu	general name for a boat
picul	unit of weight. One third of a bahar, 125 Dutch lbs
raja muda	title given to the heir apparent of a Malay state
Sulawesi	Celebes
syahbandar	harbor master
temenggung	third minister in a Malay court

Bibliography[1]

ARCHIVAL SOURCES

ALGEMEEN RIJKSARCHIEF, THE HAGUE.

Overgekomen Brieven uit Batavia, 1700–95.
- a. Malacca to Batavia; letters and papers from Malacca to the governor-general in council.
- b. Generale Missiven; letters from the governor-general in council to the Directors in the Netherlands.

Batavia's Uitgaande Briefboeken, 1641–1784. [Batavia to Malacca. Letters from the governor-general in council to Malacca.]

INDIA OFFICE LIBRARY, LONDON.

Straits Settlement Records.
Java Factory Records, vols. 1, 7.
Marine Factory Records L/MAR/600/18
                                      L/MAR/600/19
                                      L/MAR/8 438 GH

BRITISH MUSEUM

Add. Ms. 18,989. Journal of a Voyage to the East Indies, 1689–1693.

Add. Ms. 29,210. The Port of Malacca, its strength, situation, and the utility arising from that settlement was it in the possession of the English East India Company.

1. The main primary sources consulted were the letters of the Dutch East India Company [VOC], preserved in the Algemeen Rijksarchief [General State archives] of The Hague in the Netherlands. I consulted these resources both in person in The Hague and on microfilm copies obtained from the collection held in the University of the Library of Singapore. The numbers prefixed Kol. Arch. are register numbers; in a few cases this number was not available to me, because the material I used was a microfilm copy. When I have not had access to the archival number, I have quoted the nature and date of the document (e.g. Batavia to Malacca, 15 June, 1745.)

Add. Ms. 29,133. Francis Light to Governor-General Warren Hastings, (17 January 1772.)

Add. Ms. 29,164. Thomas Forrest to Governor-General Warren Hasting, (1784.)

Add. Ms. 29,166. Thomas Forrest to Governor-General Warren Hasting.

Add. Ms. 33,360. Some Papers of John Leeds, (1702–06).

Add. Ms. 34,466. Thomas Forrest to Governor-General Warren Hasting.

BOOKS AND ARTICLES

Ali al-Haji Riau, Raja. *Tuhfat al-Nafis*. Singapura, 1965.

Ali Haji ibn Ahmad, Raja. *The Precious Gift* (Tuhfat al-Nafis), annotated trans. by Virginia Matheson and Barbara Watson Andaya. Kuala Lumpur, 1982.

Andaya, Barbara Watson. "An Examination of the Sources Concerning the Reign of Sultan Mansur Shah of Trengganu, 1741–1793." *JMBRAS* 49.2 (1976): 80–106.

———. "The Installation of the First Sultan of Selangor in 1766." *JMBRAS* 47.1 (1974): 41–57.

———. "Malacca under the Dutch, 1641–1795." in Sandu and Wheatley, 195–240.

———. "The Nature of the State in 18th Century Perak." In Reid and Castles, 22–35.

———. *Perak, the Abode of Grace*. Kuala Lumpur, 1979.

———. "The Role of the Anak Raja in Malay History: a Case Study from Eighteenth-Century Kedah." *JSEAS* 7.2 (1976): 162–86.

Andaya, Barbara Watson and Virginia Matheson. "Islamic Thought and Malay Tradition—The Writings of Raja Ali Haji of Riau, (ca. 1809–1870)." In Reid and D. Marr, *Perceptions of the Past in Southeast Asia,* 108–28. Kuala Lumpur, 1979.

Andaya, Leonard Y. *The Heritage of Arung Palakka: A History of South Sulawesi [Celebes] in the Seventeenth Century*. The Hague 1981.

———. *The Kingdom of Johor, 1641–1728*. Kuala Lumpur, 1975.

———. "Raja Kecil and the Minangkabau conquest of Johor in 1718," *JMBRAS* 45.2 (1972): 51–75.

Anderson, James N. and Walter T. Vorster. "In Search of Melaka's Hinterlands: Beyond the Entrepôt." In Dilip Basu, *The Rise and Growth of Colonial Port Cities in Asia,* 1–5. Santa Cruz, 1979.

Anderson, John, *Acheen and the Ports on the North and East Coast of Sumatra, with incidental Notices of the Trade in the Eastern Seas and the Aggressions of the Dutch*. 1840. London, 1971.

———. *Mission to the East Coast of Sumatra in 1823*. 1826. London, 1971.

———. "Political and Commercial Considerations Relative to the Malayan Peninsula and the British Settlements in the Straits of Malacca." 1824. *JMBRAS* 35.4 (1962).

Arasaratnam, S. "Baron Van Imhoff and Dutch Policy in Ceylon 1736–1740." *BKI* 118.3 (1962): 454–68.

———. "The Dutch East India Co. and Its Coromandel Trade, 1700–1740." BKI 123.3 (1967): 325–47.

———. "Indian Merchants and Their Trading Methods (circa 1700)." *Indian Economic and Social History Review*, 3.1 (1966): 85–95.

———. "Monopoly and Free Trade in Dutch Asiatic Policy—Debate and Controversy within the VOC." *JSEAS*, 4.1 (1973): 1–15.

———. "Some Notes on the Dutch in Malacca and the Indo-Malayan Trade, 1641–1700," *JSEAH* 10.3 (1969): 480–90.

Baane, J. C. *Reis door Een gedeelte van de Nederlands Bezittingen in Ooste-Indisch.* Amsterdam, 1824.

Bassett, D. K. "Anglo-Malay Relations, 1786–1795." *JMBRAS* 38.2 (1965): 183–212.

———. "British Commercial and Strategic Interest in the Malay Peninsula during the Late 18th Century." In Bastin and Roolvink, 122–140. Oxford, 1964.

———. "British Trade and Policy in Indonesia, 1760–1772." *BKI* 120.3 (1964): 197–223.

———. "Changes in the Pattern of Malay Politics, 1629–1655." *JSEAH* 10.3 (1969): 429–52.

———. "The Surrender of Dutch Malacca." *BKI* 117.3 (1961): 344–58.

———. "Thomas Forrest, an 18th Century Mariner." *JMBRAS* 34.2 (1961): 106–21.

Bastin, John Sturgus. *The Changing Pattern of the Early Southeast Asian Pepper Trade.* University of Malaya, Papers on Southeast Asian Subjects, No. 1. Kuala Lumpur, 1960.

———. "Problems of Personality in the Reinterpretation of Modern Malay History." In Bastin and Roolvink, 141–55.

Bastin, John Sturgus, and Pauline Rohatgi. *Prints of Southeast Asia in the India Office Library.* London, 1979.

Bastin, John Sturgus, and R. Roolvink, eds. *Malaysian and Indonesian Studies.* Oxford, 1964.

Beeckman, Daniel. *A Voyage to the Island of Borneo . . . with a Description of the Said Island . . . together with the reestablishment of the English Trade there, Ano. 1714. Also, a Description of the Islands of Canary, Cape Verd, Java, Madura.* London, 1718.

Begbie, P. J. *The Malayan Peninsula.* Madras, 1834. Oxford, 1967.

Beknopte Encyclopaedie van Nederlandsche-Indie. The Hague and Leiden, 1921.

Blagden, C. O. "Report of Governor Balthasar Bort on Malacca: 1678." *JMBRAS* 5.1 (1927): 1–367.

Blundell, E. A. "Notices of the History and Present Condition of Malacca." *JIA* 2 (1848): 726–54.

Bonney, R. "Francis Light and Penang." *JMBRAS* 38.1 (1965): 135–58.

————. *Kedah*. Kuala Lumpur, 1971.

Bowrey, Thomas. *A Geographical Account of the Countries Round the Bay of Bengal, 1669 to 1679*. Ed. R. C. Temple. Hakluyt Society, Second Series, Vol. 12. Cambridge, 1903.

Boxer, C. R. *The Dutch Seaborne Empire, 1600–1800*. London, 1965.

————. *Jan Compagnie in War and Peace, 1602–1799. A Short History of the Dutch East India Company*. Hong Kong, 1979.

Bronson, Bennet. "Exchange at the Upstream and Downstream Ends: Notes towards a Functional Model of the Coastal State in Southeast Asia." In Karl L. Hutterer, *Economic Exchange and Social Interaction in Southeast Asia: Perspectives from Pre-history, History and Ethnology,* 39–52. Ann Arbor, 1977.

Brown, C. C., trans. "The Sejarah Melayu." *JMBRAS* 25.2–3, (1952): 5–276.

Bruijn, Jaap R. "Shipping Patterns of the Dutch East India Co." *JSEAS* 11.2 (1980): 251–65.

Burkill, I. H. *A Dictionary of the Economic Products of the Malay Peninsula*. 2 vols. London, 1935.

Chaudhuri, K. N. *The Trading World of Asia and the East India Company*. Cambridge, 1978.

Ch'en, Jerome, and Nicholas Tarling, eds. *Studies in the Social History of China and South East Asia*. Cambridge, 1970.

Cheong, W. E. "Canton and Manila in the 18th Century—a Study of Western and Oriental Mercantilist Instruments and Controls of Trade." In Ch'en and Tarling, 267–87.

Chijs, J. A. van der. ed. *Dagh-Register, Gehouden in't Casteel Batavia, 1624–1682*. The Hague and Batavia, 1896–1919.

————. *Nederlandsch-Indisch Plakaatboek, 1602–1811*. 17 vol. Batavia and The Hague, 1885–1900.

————. Realia. Register van de Generale Resolutien van het Kasteel Batavia, 1632–1805. 3 vols. Leiden, 1882–1886.

Clodd, H. P. *Malaya's First British Pioneer; The Life of Francis Light*. London, 1948.

Coates, W. H. *The Old "Country Trade" of the East Indies*. London, 1911.

Colenbrander, H. T. *Koloniale Gescheidenis*. 3 vols. The Hague, 1925.

Coolhaas, W. Ph. "Dutch Contributors to the Historiography of Colonial Activity in the 18th and 19th Centuries." In D. G. E. Hall, *Historians of Southeast Asia,* 225–35. Oxford 1961.

————. *Generale Missiven van Gouverneurs-Generaal en Raden aan Heren XVII der Verenigde Oostindische Compagnie*. 7 vols. (1610–1725). The Hague, 1964–1979.

————. "Malacca under Jan van Riebeck." *JMBRAS* 38.2 (1965): 173–82.

Crawfurd, John. *A Descriptive Dictionary of the Indian Islands and Adjacent Countries*. London, 1856.

————. *History of the Indian Archipelago*. 3 vols., Edinburgh, 1820.

Culan bin Raja Hamid, Raja. *Misa Melayu.* Kuala Lumpur, 1966.

Dalrymple, Alexander. *Oriental Repertory.* 2 vols. London, 1793.

Dam, Pieter van. *Beschryvinge van de Oostindische Compagnie.* 3 vols. The Hague, 1927–1943.Dampier, William. *A New Voyage Around the World.* London, 1927.

————. *Voyages and Discoveries.* London, 1931.

Das Gupta, Arun Kumar. "Acheh in Indonesian Trade and Politics: 1600–1641." Ph.D. diss., Cornell, 1962.

————. "Acheh in the Seventeenth Century Asian Trade." *Bengal Past and Present,* 81.1 (1962): 37–49.

Das Gupta, A. R. *Malabar in Asian Trade, 1740–1800.* Cambridge, 1967.

Davies, D. W. *A Primer of Dutch 17th Century Overseas Trade.* The Hague, 1961.

Diffie, W. Bailey, and George D. Winius, *Foundations of the Portuguese Empire, 1415–1580.* Minneapolis, 1977.

Dodwell, H. D. *A Calendar of Madras Dispatches 1745–1765.* 2 vols. Madras, 1930.

Dunmore, John, trans. "French Visitors to Trengganu in the 18th Century." *JMBRAS* 46.1 (1973): 145–60.

Earl, G. W. *The Eastern Seas, or Voyages and Adventures in the Indian Archipelago.* London, 1837.

————. "The Trading Ports of the Indian Archipelago: Asahan." *JIA* 4 (1850): 493–94.

Encyclopaedie van Nederlandsche-Indie. 2nd ed. 4 vols plus 4 supp. vols. The Hague and Leiden, 1917–1939.

Forrest, Thomas. *A Voyage from Calcutta to the Mergui Archipelago.* London, 1792.

————. *A Voyage to New Guinea and the Moluccas from Balambangan.* 2nd ed. London, 1780.

Furber, Holden. *John Company at Work—A Study of European Expansion in India in the Late 18th Century.* Harvard Historical Studies 55. Cambridge, 1948.

————. *Rival Empires of Trade in the Orient, 1600–1800.* Minneapolis, 1976.

Geyl, Pieter. *The Netherlands in the 17th Century. Part One, 1609–1648.* 2nd ed. New York, 1961. *Part Two, 1648–1715.* New York, 1964.

Glamann, Kristoff. *Dutch-Asiatic Trade, 1620–1740.* Copenhagen and The Hague, 1958.

Godée Molsbergen, E. C. "De Nederlandsch Oostindische in de achttiende eeuw." In F. W Stapel ed., *Geschiedenis van Nederlandsch Indie,* vol. 4. Amsterdam 1939.

Gullick, J. M. *A History of Selangor, 1742–1957.* Malay Historical Series, 1. Singapore, 1960.

————. *Indigenous Political Systems of Western Malaya.* London, 1958.

Hall, D. G. E. *Atlas of South-East Asia.* Amsterdam, 1964.

————. *Historians of South-East Asia.* Oxford, 1961.

————. *A History of South-East Asia.* 3rd ed. London, 1970.

Hamilton, Alexander. *A New Account of the East Indies.* 2 vols. London, 1930.

Harlow, V. *The Founding of the Second British Empire, 1763–1793.* 2. London, 1964.

Harrison, Brian, trans. "Malacca in the 18th century: Two Dutch Governors' Reports." *JMBRAS,* 27.1 (1954): 24–34.

————. "Trade in the Straits of Malacca in 1785: a memorandum (by P. G. de Bruijn, Governor of Malacca)." *JMBRAS,* 26.1 (1953): 56–62.

Heeres, J. E. "De 'Consideratien' van Van Imhoff." *BKI.* 66 (1912): 441–621.

Heeres, J. E. and F. W. Stapel. *Corpus Diplomaticum Neerlando-Indicum, 1596–1799,* The Hague, 1907–1955.

Hedges, E. S. *Tin in Social and Economic History.* London, 1964.

Hervey, D. F. A., "Malacca in the 18th Century." *JSBRAS* 12 (1883): 261–67.

————. "Valentijn's Description of Malacca." *JSBRAS* 13 (1884): 49–74; 15 (1885): 119–38; 16 (1885): 289–301; 17 (1886): 117–49; and 22 (1890): 225–46.

Hill, S. C. "Malay Piracy in the late 18th and early 19th Centuries." *Indian Antiquary* 49(1920): 78–83, 97–98, 117–22. 56 (1927): 178–81.

Hoffman, J. E. "Early Policies in the Malacca Jurisdiction of the United East India Company: The Malay Peninsula and the Netherlands East Indies Attachment." *JSEAS,* 3.1 (1972): 1–38.

Hughes, T. D., trans. "A Portuguese Account of Johore." *JMBRAS* 13.2 (1935): 110–56.

Hullu, J. de. "Van Braam Houckgeest's Memorie over Malakka en den Tinhandel aldaar (1790)." *BKI* 76 (1920): 284–309.

————. "De Engelschen op Poeloe Pinang en de Tinhandel der Nederlandsche Oost-Indische Compagnie in 1788." *BKI* 77 (1921): 605–14.

————. "De Instelling van de Commissie voor de Handel der Ooste-Indische Compagnie op China in 1756." *BKI* 79 (1923): 523–45.

Irwin, Graham W. "The Dutch and the Tin Trade of Malaya in the 17th Century." In Ch'en and Tarling, 267–87.

————. "Governor Couperus and the Surrender of Malacca, 1795." *JMBRAS* 29.3 (1956): 86–133.

————. "Melaka Fort." in Sandu and Wheatley, 1, 782–805.

————. "University of Singapore Library Dutch Archives Microfilm Collection." In K. G. Tregonning ed., *Malaysian Historical Sources,* 129–30. Singapore, 1962.

Kathirithamby-Wells, J. "Achehnese Control over West Sumatra up to the Treaty of Painan, 1663." *JSEAH* 10.3 (1969): 453–79.

————. *The British West Sumatran Presidency (1760–1785). Problems of Early Colonial Enterprise.* Kuala Lumpur, 1977.

————. "A Survey of the Effects of British Influence on Indigenous Authority in Southwest Sumatra (1685-1824)." *BKI* 129.2-3 (1973): 239–68.

Koenig, J. C. "Journal of a Voyage from India to Siam and Malacca in 1779." JSBRAS 26 (January 1894): 58–201, and 27 (October 1894): 57–133.

Kratz, Ernst Ulrich. *Peringatan Sejarah Negeri Johor. Eine Malaische Quelle zur Geschicte Johors im 18 Jahrhundrert.* Weisbaden, 1973.

Lennon, Captain Walter Caulfield. "Journal of a Voyage through the Straits of Malacca on an Expedition to the Molucca Islands." *JSBRAS* 7 (June 1881): 51–74.

Leupe, P. A. "The Siege and Capture of Malacca from the Portuguese in 1640–1641." *JMBRAS* 14.1 (1936): 1–176.

Leur, J. C. van. *Indonesian Trade and Society.* The Hague and Bandung, 1955.

Lewis, Dianne N. "The Dutch East India Company and the Straits of Malacca, 1700–1784." Ph.D. diss., Australian National University. Canberra, 1970.

———. "The Growth of the Country Trade to the Straits of Malacca, 1760-1777." *JMBRAS* 43.2 (1970): 114–30.

———. "Kedah; the Development of a Malay State." In Reid and Castles, 36–43.

———. "The Last Malay Raja Muda of Johor." JSEAS 13.2 (1982): 221–35.

———. "The Tin Trade in the Malay Peninsula during the 18th Century." *New Zealand Journal of History* 3.1 (1969): 52–69.

Light, Francis. "A Letter from Captain Light to Lord Cornwallis, dated 20th June 1788." *JMBRAS* 26.1 (1938): 115–22.

Linehan, W. *A History of Pahang.* 1936. MBRAS Reprint, 2. Kuala Lumpur, 1973.

Lockyer, C. *An Account of the Trade in India.* London, 1711.

Lombard, Denys. *Le Sultanate D'Atjeh au Temps D'Iskandar Muda.* Ecole Francais D'Extreme Orient Publications, vol. 61. Paris, 1967.

Louhizen, J. van. *The Dutch East India Company and Mysore.* The Hague, 1961.

McRoberts, R. W. "An Examination of the Fall of Malacca in 1511." *JMBRAS* 57.1 (1984): 26–39.

Marsden, William. *The History of Sumatra; Containing an Account of the Government, Laws, Customs and Manners of the Native Inhabitants.* 3rd ed. London, 1811.

Matheson, Virginia. "The Tuhfat al-Nafis; Structure and Sources." *BKI* 127.3 (1971): 375–92.

———. "Concepts of State in the *Tuhfat al Nafis.*" In Reid and Castles, 12–21.

———. "Concepts of Malay Ethos in Indigenous Malay Writings." *JSEAS* 10.2 (1979): 351–71.

Maxwell, W. E. "The Dutch in Perak." *JSBRAS* 10 (1882): 245–68.

———. "Dutch Occupation of the Dindings." *JSBRAS* 11, (1883): 169.

———. "The History of Perak from Native Sources." *JSBRAS* 9, (1882): 85–108.

———. "The History of Perak from Native Sources." *JSBRAS* 14 (1885): 305–32.

————. "Notes on Two Perak Manuscripts." *JSBRAS* 2 (1878): 83–193.

————. "Raja Haji." *JSBRAS* 22 (1890):173–224.

Meilink-Roelofsz, M. A. P. *Asian Trade and European Influence in the Indonesian Archipelago between 1500 and about 1630.* The Hague, 1962.

————. "Sources in the General State Archives in The Hague relating to the History of East Asia between c.1600 and c.1800." International Conference on Asian History, Paper 5. Hong Kong 1964.

Milburn, W. and J. Thornton. *Oriental Commerce; or the East India Trader's Complete Guide.* 2 vols. London, 1825.

Milner, A. C. *KERAJAAN; Malay Political Culture on the Eve of Colonial Rule.* Tucson, 1982.

Moreland, W. H. "Indian Exports of Cotton Goods in the Seventeenth Century." *Indian Journal of Economics* 5.3 (1925): 225–45.

Morse, H. B. "The Provision of Funds for the East India Company's Trade at Canton during the Eighteenth Century." *JRAS* (April 1922): 227–54.

Mossel, Jacob. *Memorien nopens den Staat der VOC.* 2 vols. Batavia, 1753, 1755.

Netscher, E. "Beschrijving van een gedeelte der Residentie Riouw." *TBG* 2 (1854): 108–270.

————. *De Nederlanders in Djohor en Siak, 1602–1865.* Batavia, 1870.

————. "Twee Belegeringen van Malakka, (1756–57 en 1784)." *TBG* 13 (1864): 285–362.

Newbold, T. J. *Political and Statistical Account of the British Settlements of the Straits of Malakka.* 2 vols. London, 1839.

[Noble,C. F.] *Voyage to the East Indies in 1747–1748.* London, 1762.

Osbeck, P. *A Voyage to China and the East Indies.* London, 1771.

Overbeck, Hans trans. "Sisilah Melayu dan Bugis dan Sakalian Raja-Raja-Nya." *JMBRAS* 4.3 (1926): 339–81.

Papendrecht, P. C. Hoynck van. "Some Old Private Letters from the Cape, Batavia and Malacca, (1778–1788)." *JMBRAS* 2.1 (1924): 9–24.

Pires, Tomé. *Suma Oriental.* Hakluyt Society, 2nd Series, vols. 89, 90. London 1944.

Quiason, Serafim D. *English Country trade with the Philippines, 1644–1765.* Quezon City, 1966.

Raychaudhuri, T. *Jan Company in Coromandel 1605–1690.* The Hague, 1962.

Reid, Anthony. "Trade and the Problem of Royal Power in Aceh c1550–1700." In Reid and Castles, 45–55.

Reid, Anthony, and Lance Castles. *Pre-Colonial State Systems in Southeast Asia.* Monographs of the MBRAS, 6. Kuala Lumpur, 1975.

Rhede van de Kloot, M. A. van. *De Gouverneurs-Generaal en Commisarissen-Generaal van de Nederlandsche Indie, 1610–1888.* The Hague, 1891.

Ricklefs, M. C. *Jogjakarta under Sultan Mangkubumi, 1741–1792. A History of the Division of Java.* London, 1974.

St. John, Horace. *The Indian Archipelago. Its History and Present State.* 2 vols. London, 1853.

Sandhu, K. S., and Paul Wheatley, eds. *Melaka*. Vol. 1. Kuala Lumpur, 1983.

Scott, James. "The Settlement of Penang." Edited by K.J.Fielding. *JMBRAS* 28.1 (1955): 37–51.

Sonnerat, Pierre. *Voyages aux Indes Orientales et A la Chine*. Paris, 1782.

Stavorinus, J.S. *Voyages to the East Indies, 1774–1778,* trans. by S. H. Wilcocke. London, 1789.

Suntharalingam, R. "The British in Banjarmasin, 1700–1707." *JSEAH* 4.2 (1963): 33–50.

———. *The Establishment of British Power on the West Coast of Sumatra, 1685–1716.* M.A. thesis, University of Singapore, 1961.

Surat-Surat perdjandjian antara Kesultan Riau dengan pemerintahan², Jakarta, 1970.

Tarling, Nicholas. *Anglo-Dutch Rivalry in the Malay World, 1780–1824.* Brisbane, 1962.

Trocki, Carl A. *Prince of Pirates; the Temmengongs and the Development of Johor and Singapore, 1784–1885.* Singapore, 1978.

Vaughan, Walter. *The Adventures of Five Englishmen from Pulo Condoro, in the East Indies; who were Shipwreckt upon the little Kingdom of Johore.* London, 1714.

Verhoeven, F. R. J. "The Lost Archives of Dutch Malacca, 1641–1824." *JMBRAS* 37.2 (1964): 11–27.

Valentyn, Francois. *Oud en Nieuw Oost-Indien*. 5 vols. in 8 parts. Dordrecht and Amsterdam, 1724–26.

———. "Description of Malakka and our Establishment There." trans. *JIA* 4 (1850): 696, 1747.

Wake, C. H. "Malacca's Early Kings and the Reception of Islam." *JSEAH* 5.2 (1964): 104–28.

Wijnaendts van Resandt, W. *De Gezaghebbers der Oost-Indische Compagnie op hare Buiten-Comptoiren in Azie*. Amsterdam, 1944.

Wilkinson, R. J. *An Abridged Malay-English Dictionary. (Romanised.)* Seventh Ed. London 1952.

———. *A History of the Peninsular Malays*. Singapore, 1923.

———. "The Malacca Sultanate." *JMBRAS* 13.2 (1935): 22–67.

———. *Papers on Malay Subjects*. Kuala Lumpur, 1907–25.

Winstedt, R. O. "Abdu'l Jalil, Sultan of Johore (1699–1719), Abdu'l-Jamal, Temmengong (ca. 1750) and Raffles' founding of Singapore." *JMBRAS* 11.2 (1933): 161–65.

———. *A History of Classical Malay Literature*. 2nd ed. Singapore, 1969.

———. "A History of Johore (1365–1895 A.D.)." 1932. *JMBRAS* Reprint 6 (1979): 1–162.

———. "A History of Johore, (1673–ca.1800 AD)." *JMBRAS* 10.1 (1932): 164–70.

———. *A History of Malaya*. Singapore, 1935.

———. "Notes on the History of Kedah." *JMBRAS* 14.3 (1936): 155–89.

―――. "Outline of a Malay History of Riau." *JMBRAS* 11.2 (1933): 157–60.

Winstedt, R. O., and R. J. Wilkinson. "A History of Perak." *JMBRAS* 12.1 (1934).

Wolters, O. W. *Early Indonesian Commerce.* Ithaca, 1967.

―――. *The Fall of Srivijaya in Malay History.* Kuala Lumpur, 1970.

Wong Lin Ken. *The Malayan Tin Industry to 1914.* Tucson, 1965.

Index

Monographs in International Studies
Titles Available from Ohio University Press
1995

Southeast Asia Series

No. 56 Duiker, William J. Vietnam Since the Fall of Saigon. 1989. Updated ed. 401 pp. Paper 0-89680-162-4 $20.00.

No. 64 Dardjowidjojo, Soenjono. Vocabulary Building in Indone– sian: An Advanced Reader. 1984. 664 pp. Paper 0- 89680- 118-7 $26.00.

No. 65 Errington, J. Joseph. Language and Social Change in Java: Linguistic Reflexes of Modernization in a Traditional Royal Polity. 1985. 210 pp. Paper 0-89680-120-9 $25.00.

No. 66 Tran, Tu Binh. The Red Earth: A Vietnamese Memoir of Life on a Colonial Rubber Plantation. Tr. by John Spragens. 1984. 102 pp. (SEAT*, V. 5) Paper 0-89680-119-5 $11.00.

No. 68 Syukri, Ibrahim. History of the Malay Kingdom of Patani. 1985. 135 pp. Paper 0-89680-123-3 $12.00.

No. 69 Keeler, Ward. Javanese: A Cultural Approach. 1984. 559 pp. Paper 0-89680-121-7 $25.00.

No. 70 Wilson, Constance M. and Lucien M. Hanks. Burma-Thai land Frontier Over Sixteen Decades: Three Descriptive Docu ments. 1985. 128 pp. Paper 0-89680-124-1 $11.00.

No. 71 Thomas, Lynn L. and Franz von Benda-Beckmann, eds. Change and Continuity in Minangkabau: Local, Regional, and Historical Perspectives on West Sumatra. 1985. 353 pp. Paper 0-89680-127-6 $16.00.

*SEAT= Southeast Asia Translation Project Group

No. 72 **Reid, Anthony and Oki Akira,** eds. The Japanese Experience in Indonesia: Selected Memoirs of 1942-1945. 1986. 424 pp., 20 illus. (SEAT, V. 6) Paper 0-89680-132-2 $20.00.

No. 74 **McArthur M. S. H.** Report on Brunei in 1904. Introduced and Annotated by A.V.M. Horton. 1987. 297 pp. Paper 0-89680-135-7 $15.00.

No. 75 **Lockard, Craig A.** From Kampung to City: A Social History of Kuching, Malaysia, 1820-1970. 1987. 325 pp. Paper 0-89680-136-5 $20.00.

No. 76 **McGinn, Richard,** ed. Studies in Austronesian Linguistic 1986. 516 pp. Paper 0-89680-137-3 $20.00.

No. 77 **Muego, Benjamin N.** Spectator Society: The Philippines Under Martial Rule. 1986. 232 pp. Paper 0-89680-138-1 $17.00.

No. 79 **Walton, Susan Pratt.** Mode in Javanese Music. 1987. 278 pp. Paper 0-89680-144-6 $15.00.

No. 80 **Nguyen Anh Tuan.** South Vietnam: Trial and Experience. 1987. 477 pp., tables. Paper 0-89680-141-1 $18.00.

No. 82 **Spores, John C.** Running Amok: An Historical Inquiry. 1988. 190 pp. Paper 0-89680-140-3 $13.00.

No. 83 **Malaka, Tan.** From Jail to Jail. Tr. by Helen Jarvis. 1991. 1209 pp., three volumes. (SEAT V. 8) Paper 0-89680-150-0 $55.00.

No. 84 **Devas, Nick, with Brian Binder, Anne Booth, Kenneth Davey, and Roy Kelly.** Financing Local Government in Indonesia. 1989. 360 pp. Paper 0-89680-153-5 $20.00.

No. 85 **Suryadinata, Leo.** Military Ascendancy and Political Culture: A Study of Indonesia's Golkar. 1989. 235 pp., illus., glossary, append., index, bibliog. Paper 0-89680-154-3 $18.00.

No. 86 Williams, Michael. Communism, Religion, and Revolt in Banten in the Early Twentieth Century. 1990. 390 pp. Paper 0-89680-155-1 $14.00.

No. 87 Hudak, Thomas. The Indigenization of Pali Meters in Thai Poetry. 1990. 247 pp. Paper 0-89680-159-4 $15.00.

No. 88 Lay, Ma Ma. Not Out of Hate: A Novel of Burma. Tr. by Margaret Aung-Thwin. Ed. by William Frederick. 1991. 260 pp. (SEAT V. 9) Paper 0-89680-167-5 $20.00.

No. 89 Anwar, Chairil. The Voice of the Night: Complete Poetry and Prose of Chairil Anwar . 1992. Revised Edition. Tr. by Burton Raffel. 196 pp. Paper 0-89680-170-5 $20.00.

No. 90 Hudak, Thomas John, tr., The Tale of Prince Samuttakote: A Buddhist Epic from Thailand. 1993. 230 pp. Paper 0-89680-174-8 $20.00.

No. 91 Roskies, D.M., ed. Text/Politics in Island Southeast Asia: Essays in Interpretation. 1993. 330 pp. Paper 0-89680-175-6 $25.00.

No. 92 Schenkhuizen, Marguérite, translated by Lizelot Stout van Balgooy. Memoirs of an Indo Woman: Twentieth-Century Life in the East Indies and Abroad. 1993. 312pp. Paper 0-89680-178-0 $23.00

No. 93 Salleh, Muhammad Haji. Beyond the Archipelago: Selected Poems. 1995. 247pp. Paper 0-89680-181-0 $20.00.

No. 94 Federspiel, Howard M. A Dictionary of Indonesian Islam. 1995. 327 pp. Paper 0-89680-182-9 $25.00.

Africa Series

No. 43 **Harik, Elsa M. and Donald G. Schilling.** The Politics of Educa
tion in Colonial Algeria and Kenya. 1984. 102 pp. Paper 0-89680-
117-9 $12.50.

No. 45 **Keto, C. Tsehloane.** American-South African Relations 1784-
1980: Review and Select Bibliography. 1985. 169 pp. Paper 0-
89680-128-4 $11.00.

No. 46 **Burness, Don,** ed. Wanasema: Conversations with African
Writers. 1985. 103 pp. Paper 0-89680-129-2 $11.00.

No. 47 **Switzer, Les.** Media and Dependency in South Africa: A Case
Study of the Press and the Ciskei "Homeland". 1985. 97 pp.
Paper 0-89680-130-6 $10.00.

No. 49 **Hart, Ursula Kingsmill.** Two Ladies of Colonial Algeria: The
Lives and Times of Aurelie Picard and Isabelle Eberhardt. 1987.
153 pp. Paper 0-89680-143-8 $11.00.

No. 51 **Clayton, Anthony and David Killingray.** Khaki and Blue:
Military and Police in British Colonial Africa. 1989. 347 pp.
Paper 0-89680-147-0 $20.00.

No. 52 **Northrup, David.** Beyond the Bend in the River: African Labor
in Eastern Zaire, 1864-1940. 1988. 282 pp. Paper 0-89680-151-9
$15.00.

No. 53 **Makinde, M. Akin.** African Philosophy, Culture, and Traditional
Medicine. 1988. 172 pp. Paper 0-89680-152-7 $16.00.

No. 54 **Parson, Jack,** ed. Succession to High Office in Botswana: Three
Case Studies. 1990. 455 pp. Paper 0-89680-157-8 $20.00.

No.56 **Staudinger, Paul.** In the Heart of the Hausa States. Tr. by Johanna
E. Moody. Foreword by Paul Lovejoy. 1990. In two volumes. 469
+ 224 pp.,maps, apps. Paper 0-89680-160-8 (2 vols.) $35.00.

No. 57 **Sikainga, Ahmad Alawad.** The Western Bahr Al-Ghazal under
British Rule, 1898-1956. 1991. 195 pp. Paper 0-89680-161-6
$15.00

No. 58 Wilson, Louis E. The Krobo People of Ghana to 1892: A Political and Social History. 1991. 285 pp. Paper 0-89680-164-0 $20.00.

No. 59 du Toit, Brian M. Cannabis, Alcohol, and the South African Student: Adolescent Drug Use, 1974-1985. 1991. 176 pp., notes, tables. Paper 0-89680-166-7 $17.00.

No. 60 Falola, Toyin and Dennis Itavyar, eds. The Political Economy of Health in Africa. 1992. 258 pp., notes. Paper 0-89680-168-3 $17.00.

No. 61 Kiros, Tedros. Moral Philosophy and Development: The Human Condition in Africa.1992. 199 pp., notes. Paper. 0-89680-171-3 $20.00.

No. 62 Burness, Don. Echoes of the Sunbird: An Anthology of Contemporary African Poetry. 1993. 198pp. Paper 0-89680-173-X $17.00.

No. 63 Glew, Robert S. and Chaibon Babalé. Hausa Folktales from Niger. 1993. 100pp. Paper 0-89680-176-4 $15.00.

No. 64 Nelson, Samuel H. Colonialism in the Congo Basin 1880-1940. 1993. 248 pp. Paper 089680-180-2 $23.00.

Latin America Series

No. 9 Tata, Robert J. Structural Changes in Puerto Rico's Economy: 1947-1976. 1981. 118 pp. Paper 0-89680-107-1 $12.00.

No. 12 Wallace, Brian F. Ownership and Development: A Comparison of Domestic and Foreign Firms in Colombian Manufacturing. 1987. 185 pp. Paper 0-89680-145-4 $10.00.

No. 13 Henderson, James D. Conservative Thought in Latin America The Ideas of Laureo Gomez. 1988. 229 pp. Paper 0-89680-148-9 $16.00.

No. 16 Alexander, Robert J. Juscelino Kubitschek and the Development of Brazil. 1991. 500 pp., notes, bibliog. Paper 0-89680-163-2 $25.00.

No. 17 Mijeski, Kenneth J., ed. The Nicaraguan Constitution of 1987: English Translation and Commentary. 1991. 355 pp. Paper 0-89680-165-9 $25.00.

No. 18 Finnegan, Pamela. The Tension of Paradox: Jose Donoso's *The Obscene Bird of Night* as Spiritual Exercises. 1992. 204 pp. Paper 0-89680-169-1 $15.00.

No. 19 Kim, Sung Ho and Thomas W. Walker, eds. Perspectives on War and Peace in Central America. 1992. 155 pp., notes, bibliog. Paper 0-89680-172-1 $17.00.

No. 20 Becker, Marc. Mariategui and Latin American Marxist Theory. 1993. 239 pp. Paper 0-89680-177-2 $20.00.

No. 21 Boschetto-Sandoval, Sandra M. and Marcia Phillips McGowan, eds. Claribel Alegria and Central American Literature. 1994. 263 pp., illus. Paper 0-89680-179-9 $20.00.

No. 22 Zimmerman, Marc. Literature and Resistance in Guatemala: Textual Modes and Cultural Politics from El Señor Presidente to Rigoberta Menchú. 1995. 2 volume set 320 + 370 pp., notes, bibliog. Paper 0-89680-183-7 $40.00.

ORDERING INFORMATION

Individuals are encouraged to patronize local bookstores wherever possible. Orders for titles in the Monographs in International Studies may be placed directly through the Ohio University Press, Scott Quadrangle, Athens, Ohio 45701-2979. Individuals should remit payment by check, VISA, or MasterCard. * Those ordering from the United Kingdom, Continental Europe, the Middle East, and Africa should order through Academic and University Publishers Group, 1 Gower Street, London WC1E, England. Orders from the Pacific Region, Asia, Australia, and New Zealand should be sent to East-West Export Books, c/o the University of Hawaii Press, 2840 Kolowalu Street, Honolulu, Hawaii 96822, USA.

Individuals ordering from ouside of the U.S. should remit in U.S. funds to Ohio University Press either by International Money Order or by a check drawn on a U.S. bank.** Most out-of-print titles may be ordered from University Microfilms, Inc., 300 North Zeeb Road, Ann Arbor, Michigan 48106, USA.

Prices are subject to change without notice.

* Please add $3.50 for the first book and $.75 for each additional book for shipping and handling.

** Outside the U.S please add $4.50 for the first book and $.75 for each additional book.

DATE DUE

GAYLORD			PRINTED IN U.S.A.